UNSHAKEABLE
Confidence

Jen Baker

CWR

Copyright © Jen Baker, 2018

Published 2018 by CWR, Waverley Abbey House, Waverley Lane, Farnham, Surrey GU9 8EP, UK.

CWR is a Registered Charity – Number 294387 and a Limited Company registered in England – Registration Number 1990308.

The right of Jen Baker to be identified as the author of this work has been asserted by her in accordance with the Copyright, Designs and Patents Act 1988.

For a list of National Distributors, visit www.cwr.org.uk/distributors

Scripture references are taken from The Holy Bible, English Standard Version Anglicised, ESVUK® Copyright ©2001 by Crossway Bibles, a division of Good News Publishers.

Other versions are marked: *The Message,* Copyright © 1993, 1994, 1995, 1996, 2000, 2001, 2002 by Eugene H. Peterson; New International Version® Anglicised, NIV® Copyright © 1979, 1984, 2011 by Biblica, Inc.®; The Amplified Bible, Classic Edition, Copyright © 1954, 1958, 1962, 1964, 1965, 1987 by the Lockman Foundation; NLT: New Living Translation, Copyright © 1996, 2004, 2015 by Tyndale House Foundation; NASB: New American Standard Bible, Copyright © 1960, 1962, 1963, 1968, 1971, 1972, 1973, 1975, 1977, 1995 by The Lockman Foundation; CEV: Contemporary English Version, Copyright © 1995 by the American Bible Society; NKJV: New King James Version, Copyright © 1982 by Thomas Nelson.

Concept development, editing, design and production by CWR.

Every effort has been made to ensure that this book contains the correct permissions and references, but if anything has been inadvertently overlooked the Publisher will be pleased to make the necessary arrangements at the first opportunity. Please contact the Publisher directly.

Cover image: unsplash.com/@brookecagle

Thank you to Estienne Photography for the author photo

Printed in the UK by Linney

ISBN: 978-1-78259-840-4

DEDICATION

This book is dedicated to Lisa
- for her courage, tenacity, wisdom, faith,
generosity, kindness and unswerving
dedication to Christ and His calling.
Your voice is powerful.

Acknowledgements

This book, more than my others, feels like a team effort. Possibly because it is my most vulnerable, sharing details of my childhood which I have not previously put in print. Remembering, and putting words to memories has emphasised afresh the truth that none of us are meant to navigate life alone.

My family – You have believed in me when I hardly believed in myself. In my lowest seasons you have been my greatest source of earthly strength. Thank you for seeing what I could not see... until I could.

My mentors – Elaine, Bev, Jeff, Sylvia... Thank you for your authenticity, love, challenge and example. Your wisdom has been invaluable to me.

My US friends – Writing a list is always dangerous! But I would be remiss not to mention Amber, my oldest and dearest friend in the US. Our friendship has stood the test of time and many ups and downs. The fact that you are an Anglophile who owns her own scone business is simply the stamp of heaven on its authenticity – I am your friend for life, and beyond. And for the many others too numerous to name, thank you for cheering me on, often from a distance, showing that the family of God far exceeds geographical borders. I love you.

My UK tribe – Beth, Phil, Ken, Jane, Harry, Esther, Amanda, Dave, Karen, Sharon, Jon, Andrea, Laura, Susan, Estienne, Helen, Susie (forgive me if I've missed a name here – I blame it on not enough coffee)… thank you. Just… thank you.

Bath City Church – I'm so blessed to be part of the family. Thank you for being you.

My prayer warriors – Those in my 'inner circle', Kay, Amanda, my prayer team and the many others I do not know by name who pray for me... *thank you* for each and every prayer. You cannot know the depth of my gratitude for the times you have brought me before the throne of heaven. This book is yours as much as mine.

My partners – *Thank you* for supporting me both financially and by believing in this ministry. This journey is as much yours as it is mine and I am tremendously excited for the future of the ministry and the many people we can reach with the gospel of Christ. I pray that the Lord will return to you all you've given through blessings beyond what you could dream or imagine!

Amy Boucher Pye – You have been a solid rock of wisdom, support, prayer, encouragement, guidance and honesty throughout this process. I cannot thank you enough for cheering me on. And the fact that you are an American brings a comfort I didn't know I was looking for in a friend. Thank you.

Cathy Madavan – You are a source of inspiration, fun, wisdom and encouragement. Thank you for letting me join your journey and for taking part in mine – it is much more fun doing this together. The fact that we were both writing like mad women the final week made it far more palatable... we made it! #chocolate

CWR – We did it again! To the whole team at CWR, you are becoming like family. Thank you for making a (sometimes) arduous project more enjoyable. You are always a pleasure to work with and your words of encouragement keep me going on the tough days! A special mention to Lynette Brooks for her support, encouragement, patience, wisdom and overall kindness and Lucy Harris for making me sound better than I am. You are gems.

And finally, but most importantly, thank You Lord for Your unending patience, grace, guidance and love toward an insecure, terrified, lonely dreamer of a girl.
I am who I am because of You.
I love You.

Contents

Introduction

An iconic symbol of Russia has to be the wooden Russian dolls – beautiful, hand-painted creations which, when opened, reveal a smaller figurine inside, and upon opening that one, an even tinier one emerges… and on it goes until you find a miniature child at the core of the little Russian family. Hand-crafted and originally designed, these unique creations could loosely symbolise our lives as well: the presentation of an outward image for the world to see, while safely tucked inside lie a multitude of hidden layers, which when combined, create the whole person.

Unshakeable confidence also resembles the dolls – layers unveiled throughout the changing seasons of life. The deeper our confidence grows, the more layers are revealed until – at the core – we discover our true identity made in the likeness of Christ Himself. Here we realise that our outward self is only a 'shell', housing the inner beauty of a spiritual being united with her Creator. It is that inward self – the spirit part of our being – that carries the keys to freedom and a healthy, strong, confident life.

For years I only saw the outer shell, and it nearly killed me.

Lying immobile on the bathroom floor, I wondered if this was the way my life would end.

Having just made myself throw up for what felt like the hundredth time over many months, I now lay paralysed, numb with exhaustion and unable to move. Approximately 15 minutes had passed when, slipping in and out of consciousness, I heard a voice – not audibly, but with authority – saying that if I attempted to be sick again, I would die.

I thought to myself, *Finally.*

Once movement returned, I used my arms to pull myself the final few feet to the toilet, thoughts of hopelessness assailing my every movement. I lifted my head to the basin, thinking how pathetic I must have looked, and took a moment to pause with my fingers perilously close to my mouth, contemplating the ramifications of my decision. It was the lowest point of my life and I felt like a complete failure… at only 16 years of age.

Willing myself to do it, I suddenly relented.

I couldn't follow through with it.

Failing at self-destruction takes a person to a new low.

Dragging myself out of the bathroom I found a phonebook, dialled the first counsellor's number that I saw, and quietly whimpered, 'Please… I need help.'

I periodically think back to that moment, uncertain how that girl could have become the woman I see in the mirror today. I feel pity, sadness and deep compassion for a girl in such despair, yet also admiration at the brave choice that girl made to live – not only in body, but as a whole person. I remember hanging up the phone with the counsellor's office and saying to myself, *You're such a failure, you couldn't even kill yourself successfully.*

What I didn't realise was that I had made the bravest choice anyone can make – choosing life over death, peace over pain and freedom over bondage. It is a choice we can all make, in small and large measures, every day of our lives. That decision began defining the rest of my life, and continues to define every word in this book.

Here you will find four sections: Foundational Keys, Immovable Truths, Dangerous Lies and Brilliant Future. Each section builds upon the others, taking us through my own journey of healing. My goal is to give you tools which can be used to strengthen the next step in your own personal journey towards freedom.

As you read, I pray the presence of the Holy Spirit will walk with you, leading you towards truth, uncovering the lies and revealing the 'you' beautifully designed since the beginning of time: a woman who is unshakeable in the confidence of her calling, her creation and her King.

Part One

FOUNDATIONAL KEYS

Power of Choice

Anyone other than me

'choose for yourselves this day whom you will serve... But as for me and my household, we will serve the LORD.' **(Josh. 24:15, NIV)**

I am beautiful, I am smart. I am beautiful, I am smart. I am... (sigh)... ugly, I am stupid.

I remember the day like it was yesterday, walking the quiet, American Midwest streets trying to convince myself of something I was not at all convinced of – my own worth. Earlier that morning I had looked with tremendous hatred at the reflection staring back at me from the mirror, longing to be anyone other than Jen Baker. My eyelashes were too blonde, my arms and legs gangly and thin, my neck was like a giraffe's and my chest... well, let's just say I'm at the front end of the alphabet. In that moment all I could see was someone outwardly ugly and inwardly boring.

Sighing, I remembered an event not long before, on my first attempt at snuffing out my young life, when I had taken several aspirins, hoping they would end my pain – only to receive a long nap as a result. Nobody even knew I had tried; the woods were my bed and the leaves my pillow. Being a romantic at heart, I envisioned it unfolding like a character out of a novel – she attempts to take her life in the tall grass alongside the cool water, suddenly discovered by a handsome young man who wakes her from sleep before it is too late. Sleeping Beauty I was not, and groggily waking several hours later I vacillated between relief and remorse that I was still breathing.

Maybe you can relate to feeling hopeless at a young age? Perhaps you grew up being compared to older siblings or your home life was not the idyllic childhood we see in storybooks. You may have struggled with acne, weight, isolation, anxiety or a stutter – those becoming the first narratives of your unfolding story. Or maybe your earlier chapter was tainted by abuse, someone taking advantage of you through their words or actions; or neglect – many have experienced the absence of a parent, even while present. We all have scars which brand our young lives, shaping the story we become. These wounds will either draw us further from our divine purpose or hurl us nearer heaven's destined plan. Ultimately, the choice is ours.

Walking those streets more than 30 years ago, I did the only thing I knew to do: endlessly repeat positive statements, hoping repetition would foster belief. Words carry weight, as we will see later, but only words filled with the Spirit of life can turn temporary adjustment into lasting transformation. As a teenager who did not know Christ, I would have to settle for temporary adjustment.

And that is where my story begins…

Finishing middle school and entering high school was a memorable transition for me. I decided that moving to where the big kids were gave me an opportunity to start afresh, to be someone different from who I had always been – the awkward, shy girl. I could make a new beginning, altering my reputation for the better. I had always wanted to be an actress, so the corridors of Mattawan High School became my first platform. I made a decision: every person who made eye contact with me would receive a friendly 'Hello…' and I would deliberately make eye contact with as many students and teachers as possible. Only one word adequately describes my feelings that first day: petrified.

Acute shyness had plagued me all my life, and speaking to anyone outside my immediate family brought on a feeling of terror faster than shoppers running for a new TV on Black Friday. Eye contact was allowing another to see me and I did not want anyone else viewing the ugliness I saw in the mirror each day. But now I had challenged, berated and – quite frankly – ordered myself to 'stop being so stupid', intentionally aiming to become someone different.

So… I began saying hello.

'Hi.'

'Hello.'

'Hi there.'

'Hi.'

And on it went my first day, gaining courage with each greeting, until, weeks later, I was able to speak that one simple word without turning bright red, visibly shaking, breaking into a sweat and fighting heart palpitations. I am not exaggerating – it was genuinely that awful.

Courage began at hello. One step, one change and one decision literally changed the trajectory of my life. Other students began to notice me, speak to me and invite me into their circles.

Soon I found myself navigating between the popular kids and those on the periphery. I was voted class secretary for the student board and the transformation from shy tomboy to confident, stiletto-wearing preacher began.

Not to decide is to decide

Although my confidence was growing, one area that still brought immediate 'mental paralysation' was needing to make a decision. Committing to a choice was an agonising process for many years, partly because as a very young child my options were often removed. Although my parents aimed to instill in us children a freedom to know our own minds, my mother would inadvertently take small decisions out of our hands. Following the pattern of her own upbringing, she felt choosing on our behalf would simplify matters when it came to daily tasks such as picking out our outfits or deciding on a snack. With two small children under the age of two, it is understandable why she would have done this, and for most children it probably would not have adversely affected them. Her motives were right, but the result was disempowering and unhelpful for a terribly sensitive child like myself.

Though I was not always indecisive, I preferred having someone else make my decisions. It meant the pressure was off if something went wrong and I would save myself from looking foolish if I chose poorly. Some choices were blatantly obvious when I was younger (I don't want broccoli!), but a few good options could have me deliberating in my mind for hours, heart racing with fear at the prospect of getting it wrong. As I grew older, there were times I simply opted out of choosing, thinking that was

'...*not* deciding is ultimately a decision'

a safer bet. But as I learned through the lens of adulthood, *not* deciding is ultimately a decision; and under the power of procrastination, change always increases in difficulty.

Some of you may have battled many years of insecurity or fear, but that is not God's will for your life. We were created for much more than that – each one being given gifts to use and a voice to speak. You carry purpose within you, designed to impact this world for the glory of God; and not only that – you also have a voice, designed to speak boldly in authority and truth. If we opt out of abiding by, and speaking, absolute truth, then people are left with relativism and political correctness.

Public opinion and politics will never create a kingdom culture. This is seen all too clearly in Mark 15:1–20 where Jesus stands accused before Pontius Pilate, the Roman governor at the time. After the Jews swarmed the palace demanding an audience with the governor, Pilate finally made an appearance. Joining the theatrics, he provided a spontaneous inquest to gather evidence against Jesus which would prove Him worthy of death – and found none. Ignoring his wife's warning to walk away from the whole scene, political correctness won and Pilate challenged Jesus by asking, 'What is truth?' (John 18:38). At this point Pilate found no basis to accuse Jesus (Luke 23:4), but because truth held no moral compass in his life, politics swayed him to give the people what they wanted – a death.

The impact of doubt and indecision is immense, and we will periodically revisit these themes throughout the book. They are some of the greatest killers of walking in confidence, as we read in James 1:6 where it says, 'But let him ask in faith, with no doubting, for the one who doubts is like a wave of the sea that is driven and tossed by the wind.' It is impossible to doubt and flourish in faith at the same time, simply impossible. Doubt will destroy any sense of forward movement, paralysing possibility from taking root.

'Doubt will destroy any sense of forward movement, paralysing possibility from taking root'

The rich young ruler in Mark 10:17–22 showed us this when he found the sway of finances greater than the security of faith. Tragically, his doubt surrounding provision left him grieved, missing out on a future filled with adventure. I heard one preacher say that they believed the rich young ruler was destined to fill Judas' shoes as treasurer after he betrayed Jesus. Obviously we cannot know that for certain, but I agree with the theory – quite possibly this young man turned down an opportunity to be in the inner circle of Jesus' confidantes, learning from the Messiah Himself… because he placed his confidence in the temporary, instead of trusting in the eternal.

If we are not careful, indecision will encroach on our sphere of decision making, bringing complications and confusion. God deeply values our ability to choose, therefore He leaves the greatest decision of our lives – the decision to follow Him – up to us. Love always allows the freedom of decision and choice; it never forces and it never tries to control. God's love is what ultimately empowers us to walk in greater love with others, freely knowing our boundaries and confidently making our choices.

Empowered or overpowered?

There is a vast gulf between empowered and overpowered. *Empowered* is having the ability to make choices, do things differently and affect an outcome; while *overpowered* is feeling helpless, inept and at a loss to affect change. If we find ourselves struggling in the latter category, being in Christ can enable us to make the change we desire. Heart transformation will not happen through a greater willpower or self-help book, but through revelation of our right-standing in Christ, as the Holy Spirit partners with the Word of God to change our mindset and renew our vision. Mother Teresa said, 'Be faithful in small things because it is in them that your strength lies.' The small decisions – to spend time in our Bibles, worship the Lord and watch our words – create a strength that is reliant on something beyond our self-will.

One of my favourite stories is where a woman who looked overpowered demonstrated what it means to walk empowered. We can read the story in Mark 5:25–34:

'And there was a woman who had had a discharge of blood for twelve years, and who had suffered much under many physicians, and had spent all that she had, and was no better but rather grew worse. She had heard the reports about Jesus and came up behind him in the crowd and touched his garment. For she said, "If I touch even his garments, I will be made well." And immediately the flow of blood dried up, and she felt in her body that she was healed of her disease. And Jesus, perceiving in himself that power had gone out from him, immediately turned about in the crowd

and said, "Who touched my garments?" And his disciples said to him, "You see the crowd pressing around you, and yet you say, 'Who touched me?'" And he looked round to see who had done it. But the woman, knowing what had happened to her, came in fear and trembling and fell down before him and told him the whole truth. And he said to her, "Daughter, your faith has made you well; go in peace, and be healed of your disease."

She had faced 12 years of disappointment, shame, humiliation and gradual poverty. According to Jewish law, having an issue of blood meant that anything this woman touched would become unclean and so she was not allowed into the temple for religious ceremonies. That means that this woman had not 'been to church' or had any compassionate physical contact for *12 years*. The disease had taken control of her physically and materially, yet miraculously she remained strong in faith. Instead of growing negative and complaining about 'the cards she had been dealt', she remained steadfast and hopeful about her future. Empowerment will do that. It makes choices that other people would never make, to obtain results that few people will ever see.

We must not let circumstances dictate how we view our level of spiritual authority. This precious woman intentionally pushed against the legalism of society to reach the freedom of Christ. And though the world may try to put us in a box or judge us incorrectly, in Christ we find freedom and acceptance. Jesus intentionally called her 'daughter' – in front of the disciples and the ruler of the synagogue (v34) – declaring to everyone present that this woman was acceptable before God, and therefore must be accepted both in the community and in the synagogue. From one tenacious woman we see how perseverance and a refusal to quit brought total transformation in a moment, simultaneously sowing a seed of hope for the millions of people reading her story in the years to come. It takes a decision and, as we are about to discover, even the smallest of decisions can have the greatest of impacts.

Tweaking

If you had told that suicidal teenager 30 years ago that her future included writing several books, speaking internationally on platforms, leading charities and mentoring young women, she may have believed it was possible – but not as her true self. Only by creating another character and living as someone other than myself would I have believed I could be anyone remotely successful. In fact, I remember sitting in my bedroom dreaming about who I could become, and how I needed to alter my personality in order to reach the dreams I thought were beyond my current character. In reality, only in the last few years have I *fully* begun walking in a godly confidence, without fearing the opinions of others. I am far from perfect and yes, there are still times when insecurity rears its ugly head and catches me off guard. But now I have the ability to boldly stare it down and command it with an authority I once only dreamed of holding. I am enjoying walking in my new nature, refusing to be ruled by the old one any longer. Freedom is too refreshing to remain stuck in old mindsets.

'Freedom is too refreshing to remain stuck in old mindsets'

It says in 2 Corinthians 3:18: 'And we all, with unveiled face, beholding the glory of the Lord, are being transformed into the same image from one degree of glory to another. For this comes from the Lord who is the Spirit.'

In Christ, we have *been* transformed and we are *being* transformed... simultaneously. At salvation we became a new creation (2 Cor. 5:17) when our spirit was awakened and we became fully alive in body, soul and spirit. But as I think we can all admit, there remains a bit of work to be done! Our habits, language, attitudes and belief systems may still be stuck in the old way of thinking, and those elements transform over time, becoming more Christlike as we deepen our relationship with Him. Transformation will never happen without time and intentionality: it

'Transformation will never happen without time and intentionality: it needs both'

needs both. Time without intention may bring awareness, but no real change. Intention without time can foster mere self-effort, remaining shallow and burdensome. There is a vast difference between our responsibility and God's responsibility. Too often we assume responsibility for our transformation, when that belongs to the Lord; but we abdicate responsibility for our choices, and those remain solely within our hands.

I was recently reminded of this when my Ray-Ban sunglasses needed repairing. The glasses are special to me, having received them as a spontaneous gift from a girl I mentor; yet as fashionable as they looked, I could not tilt my head without them threatening to high-jump off my face. Not being a glasses expert, I was curious how they would fix this problem without damaging the specs. Finding what looked like a trustworthy store, I boldly approached the counter, relinquishing my cherished glasses to a young man who appeared just a few years shy of puberty.

He briefly 'examined' them (ie picked them up), put one finger on either side of the nose pads… and pushed.

'That's it?' I asked.

'That's it,' he replied (smugly, I might add).

Watch it kid, I could be your mother.

A short time later I sensed that the Lord wanted to teach me a lesson. Turning my spiritual ears towards Him, I soon heard the following: 'You were looking for transformation, but only tweaking was needed.' At times we think our lives need complete transformation, an expensive and time-consuming process, when in the eyes of God, only a tweak is required. If we are intently focused on transformation (which is God's responsibility), we may miss the life-changing tweaks that occur through routine surrender. It is the consistent, everyday decisions that ultimately bring about our transformation; and it is the determination not to give up and to remain committed to obeying God's Word that makes our transformation a lasting one.

Freedom coach

If self-discipline does not come easily to you, don't worry – that's true for most of us! Thankfully, self-control is a fruit of the Spirit (Gal. 5:22–23), which takes up residence within us the moment we become a Christian. For that reason, we cannot say with integrity that we 'have no self-control' because we actually do: the issue is submission and whether or not we will submit to the Holy

Spirit's conviction and leading in order to grow this fruit. While this is not encouraging to our flesh, it should be encouraging to our soul (which is our mind, will and emotions), because this means our fleshly desires never have the final word, unless we hand it to them! God would never allow our flesh more power than His Word – that would be cruel and the complete opposite of love. He has designed us as a three-part being – body, soul and spirit – and each affects the other to its strength or to its detriment. Within that design, we can choose which of the three will have the greatest authority in our lives. Before salvation, only our body or soul could make a demand; but at the sacred moment of salvation, our spirit is given a voice – and with that voice comes the authority to affect change and develop character. We are more powerful than we know!

But character is never forged out of increased effort; it is grown out of deeper surrender. In other words, it cannot be made: it must be cultivated. The more we trust the process and the potter (Isa. 64:8), the freer He is to shape our destiny and develop our character. Once we begin to see benefits from our choices, it will inevitably increase our desire to make further healthy choices – in all areas. A strong marriage reflects a multitude of good (and often hard) choices made by both partners over many years. A healthy body is the result of saying 'no' when others have said 'yes'. (This isn't a book on healthy eating, but I would be remiss if I did not mention at the start how our physical body affects our mental outlook, and can subsequently affect our spiritual wellbeing. We read in 1 Corinthians 6:19–20: 'do you not know that your body is a temple of the Holy Spirit within you, whom you have from God?... So glorify God in your body.' This includes honouring

Him by the foods we eat and how we care for the temple He has given us.)

Developing inner health, strength and unshakeable confidence will not happen overnight, but it *can* happen, as we deliberately surrender to the truth of God's Word and the power of His grace. Take some time to reflect on your journey up to now, contemplating when the fear and insecurity first began and what an ideal confidence would look like for you. Is there anything you would like to be doing that you are not currently doing? How would you respond differently in your relationships if you walked with true (healthy) strength? Are there unfulfilled goals you would consider pursuing if you had the confidence?

I want to come alongside as a 'freedom coach' of sorts, encouraging you on your journey, believing with you for breakthrough. We can *all* be healthy, strong and empowered to fulfill God's calling on our lives when we surrender to our Lord Jesus and determine to consistently make biblical choices. As I mentioned, the most important decision is found in our relationship with Jesus Christ, choosing to make Him number one in our lives. He is the rock of our salvation and the solid foundation beneath our feet. True confidence only comes from a personal relationship with Him – one that is based on love and full acceptance from our Creator and Saviour. Knowing He loves us deeply and intimately frees us to love others in the same way. You will find on pages 149–150 a prayer of salvation and rededication. I encourage you to pray this, either alone or with a friend, if you want to start (or renew) a relationship with Christ. He adores you. He created you for a purpose. And He is eager to walk with you on this journey!

Power of Identity

Masks

'For as he thinks in his heart, so *is* he.'
(Prov. 23:7, NKJV)

My hand rested nervously on the bedroom doorknob, suddenly arrested by panic in the middle of my rush to leave... I could not remember who I was supposed to be.

Growing up, I wore many different masks. For my family I was the dramatic one who loved to tell stories and make people laugh, but for school I was the shy, friendly girl who never rocked the boat with her opinion. Behind the scenes I was a chatterbox with certain friends and a silent observer with others – letting their personality decide what mine would become. I carried my fears and insecurities like a backpack everywhere I went, masks readily available to switch according to who I was with at any given moment.

So standing at my bedroom door, I frantically searched the metaphorical pack for a mask that matched this friendship. Finally I remembered – with her I was the shy one. Façade affixed, the door swung open: outwardly, I was now covered... inwardly, I remained laid bare. To some extent, I believe we all wear masks now and again – actions saying one thing and our hearts saying another. Handing our emotions the keys of control is childish and immature, let alone irresponsible. On the other hand, maturity uses wisdom and, at times, restraint when it comes to expressing everything we feel. A benign example: as frustrating as it is following slow drivers, displaying road rage will never be a good Christian witness!

More seriously, there are times when a 'mask' must be worn to protect our children from seeing fear that would be unhealthy to process at their age, or when we put aside our own unspoken pain to help a friend who is deeply struggling. Those of us in ministry have reached a certain level of maturity when we can unreservedly minister to others, even while our own hearts are breaking. I am not talking about hiding truths or being insincere, but rather following Jesus' example: when He was confronted with a crowd of needy people in the middle of His own personal grief, He had compassion on them. In other words, He maturely set aside His private pain to help others in their time of need (Matt. 14:12–14). He was not affixing a mask out of fear, but revealing faith in a Father who would take care of Him, as He took care of others. That type of maturity is grown from knowing your true identity and walking in humility.

What is humility?

Walking in humility means we can be vulnerable, no longer striving for acceptance or approval, having received it in spades through our Creator. Matthew 11:29 (AMPC) says: 'Take My yoke upon you and learn of Me, for I am gentle (meek) and humble (lowly) in heart, and you will find rest (relief and ease and refreshment and recreation and blessed quiet) for your souls.'

Christ shows that with humility comes rest and refreshment for our souls. Pride strives, seeking to have its own way, pushing to the front. It seeks to meet its own needs before the needs of others. It is deeply concerned about perception – wanting to be recognised and admired. Humility waits patiently, doing whatever job is needed, regardless of position or title. It is not offended when others receive the applause or the credit – for it performs to an audience of one – *the* one, who bestows all true honour and glory. Though humility may look like weakness, it is beautiful strength. Brené Brown describes vulnerability this way: 'Vulnerability sounds like truth and feels like courage. Truth and courage aren't always comfortable, but they are never weakness.'[1]

True humility never gives licence to be taken advantage of or abused; that is born from insecurity. Jesus was the most humble person who ever lived. He showed humility by refusing to remain as deity only, taking on a human form and identifying with our fallen state, in order to redeem and restore us as children of God (Phil. 2:6–8). But even the cross was His decision: none of it happened without His consent. He *chose* to take our punishment and endure unimaginable agony on our behalf (John 15:13; Heb. 12:2) – revealing great strength of character and humility in the midst of humiliation.

Living in Britain, I have noticed at times a misunderstanding of kingdom humility. Here it is culturally acceptable to walk in self-deprecation – mocking oneself or intentionally dismissing any form of praise. Let me be clear – this is not humility! In fact, that type of thinking expressly opposes a kingdom mentality. Nowhere in Scripture do we see Jesus brushing aside words of praise or adoration, and certainly our Father has never said, 'Oh, please…

your worship is too much… just stop.' That is ludicrous to think, and nearly sacrilege to write! Father, Son and Holy Spirit are worthy of *all* our worship and adoration! And we are His children. While we are clearly not to be worshipped, neither are we to be dismissed. Every person has been given spiritual and natural gifts from heaven – and there is nothing wrong with acknowledging those gifts, receiving praise for them and using them for the benefit of society, which is why they were given in the first place. At the end of the day, it is not about us.

And yet… it is.

'For by the grace given to me I say to every one among you not to think of himself more highly than he ought to think, but to think with sober judgement, each according to the measure of faith that God has assigned.' (**Rom. 12:3**)

Many people believe this verse is suggesting that it is scriptural to think 'lowly' of ourselves, kicking ourselves to the end of the queue. That is *not* what it says. It says not to think of yourself *more highly than you should*… and as I heard one preacher say, it does not give us boundaries for how high we can think! I believe many women are so concerned about crossing the line that they have remained miles behind the line instead. The minute we begin to feel confident and secure, we hear that scoffing voice inside saying, 'What will people think if you do/say that?… Speaking up for yourself is being prideful and arrogant… Just be humble and take it, don't cause a scene… Who do you think you are?… Why would they want your opinion?… Posting that on social media makes you look like you're self-promoting…' And on it goes, until we gingerly retreat into the safety of silence and self-deprecation once again.

If this is a struggle for you, please take a moment to receive this: *it is OK to think highly of yourself.* God does not mind us acknowledging the natural and spiritual gifts we have received from Him, especially as we use them to bless others and further His kingdom. The balance of this is found in the words of Charles Spurgeon: 'When a man admires himself he never adores God.'[2] In other words, we are not meant to put ourselves on a pedestal of admiration – that place solely belongs to the Lord; but neither are we meant to ignore or belittle our gifts through false humility – that would criticise God's handiwork. Keeping the balance between the two helps us to avoid the extremes of both arrogance and insecurity.

Soul care

Pride could arguably be defined as the opposite of humility, so where is the line between arrogance and confidence? Ultimately, pride stems from insecurity and fear – the need to demonstrate importance in order to be accepted or approved. Humility knows its own worth and value, feeling no need to showcase before others. A humble woman never hides her talents or gifts, yet neither does she think of herself as greater than anyone else because of them.

I would imagine that many of us define confidence in terms of outward actions – how someone acts, walks, talks or appears. In fact, I did a few social media surveys asking women what word or phrase immediately came to mind when they heard the word 'confidence'. The results were fascinating! Self-acceptance was the most common theme – being oneself, whatever form that took. One woman had the courage to admit her first thought was her 'ideal body image' (which I believe many women can relate to) and a few others mentioned the ability to risk rejection and step outside their comfort zone. I was struck by how many of the answers revolved around 'self': self-esteem, knowing yourself, believing in yourself, being yourself… one person even described confidence as 'Me!'.

Is it possible to separate confidence from self? I don't believe it is, because confidence reflects an inward belief expressing itself through outward actions. But if we stop at self, haven't we limited our confidence to the realm of the soul, residing within our control alone? If we are exclusively responsible for our own confidence and soul-care, immune to the Spirit's influence, that is a tremendous amount of pressure to carry. What if, instead, our confidence was built on Spirit-led choices, not ability-led decisions? One woman on social media defined confidence as 'nothing to prove', which I found intriguing as we live in a society that thrives on performance and approval. With comparison and competition rampant in our western world, we often live to 'look good', instead of looking to 'live good'. There is a vast difference between those two and, sadly, the former outlook is far more prevalent in today's world. Modern politics crucify any leader who reveals the smallest chink in their armour, with the (alleged) weakness plastered across media platforms, bringing with it the potential destruction of their career.

'What if, instead, our confidence was built on Spirit-led choices, not ability-led decisions?'

The world sees confidence as boldly living without fear or shame, regardless of accountability or the moral impact on society. Integrity has become a relative concept and personal 'rights' have become the popular platitude whenever someone acts in a manner that conflicts with our soul's comfort zone. Once God and His Word are removed, there is no truth – no basis on which to judge what is right or wrong. This allows insecurity to masquerade as individuality, thereby creating a culture based on pride and not humility, moving us further away from our original identity. Recently I saw a social media post that said, 'I will allow the Father to meet the needs of my soul, so that I can be free from the need to perform.'[3] Healthy strength will always be connected to a strong relationship with the Saviour. In order to remain in a continual state of health, our soul must receive its affirmation and approval from the Creator, not from society or achievement. Even the most loving spouse should not be the essence of our soul's peace, as humanity cannot produce what heaven sources.

'Healthy strength will always be connected to a strong relationship with the Saviour'

Fourteen years of living in England have given me unique insight into the culture – not as a native, yet as much more than a bystander. As mentioned earlier, I have regularly observed the quintessentially British trait of self-deprecation, which is socially acceptable and culturally relevant, yet spiritually stifling and largely unbiblical. This cultural norm has influenced the (particularly British) Christian woman to her detriment, potentially making it more challenging to carry a healthy confidence in Christian circles. Over the years I have heard many women express concern that if they appear confident they will be labelled as arrogant or even worse – a feminist! Personally, I believe there is a place for feminism in the Christian world, if defined correctly and lived out biblically. (Incidentally, it looks far different from the world's typical definition of feminism.) We are not here to explore that topic, but I would highly recommend the book *Jesus Feminist*[4] if you are interested in studying this further. I encourage all of us, for the sake of those around us and the generations coming behind us, to let the Lord alone be ruler of our souls and the source of our confidence!

Ezer

I used to avoid women's conferences. Sitting in a room full of that much oestrogen and emotion was all a bit of an overkill for the choleric side of my personality. But the Lord has changed my heart and now I love speaking to groups of women, watching the Lord soften rough edges and draw out inner strength. Sorry men, but I think being a woman is the best! We are created beautifully unique with a stunning combination of gentleness and strength – soft enough to soothe the hurting, yet fierce enough to birth new life. Genesis 2:20 says, 'The man gave names to all livestock and to the birds of the heavens and to every beast of the field. But for Adam there was not found a helper fit for him.' The Hebrew word for suitable is *kenegdo*[5] and the word for helper is *ezer*.[6] I think many of us have heard the teaching on the word 'helpmeet', which focuses on a woman coming alongside a man; and many times we think of this in terms of marriage. But the word is not limited to a marriage relationship, as author Sarah Bessey (quoting Carolyn Custis James) explains:

> 'This traditional and narrow view "excludes 60 percent of females in this country [the United States] alone. How many millions of women and girls are we leaving out worldwide? Focus on the wife as her husband's helper has led to the belief that God gave primary roles and responsibilities to men, and secondary, supporting roles to women. It has led to practices that communicate that women are second-class citizens at home and in the church."'[7]

Not only is the phrase meant for all women, the placement of *kenegdo* alongside *ezer* actually means 'corresponding to him; equal and adequate to himself'.[8] We see this further explained by biblical scholar and theologian Victor Hamilton:

> '[Kenegdo] suggests that what God creates for Adam will correspond to him. Thus the new creation will be neither a superior nor an inferior, but an equal. The creation of this helper will form one half of a polarity and will be to man as the South Pole is to the North Pole.'[9]

I remember being in a pastors' meeting years ago, with 15 pastors sitting around a large boardroom table. One of the female pastors answered a question and the Senior Pastor said, in effect, 'And that, men, is the reason you must always have women at the table – they will see things from a different perspective.' We are meant to complement men, not as inferior or superior, but as equally important in the roles, beliefs, values and opinions we hold.

Sarah Bessey goes on to say:

'In the Old Testament, the word ezer appears twenty-one times in three different contexts: the creation of woman, when Israel applied for military aid, and in reference to God as Israel's helper for military purposes (in this context, ezer appears sixteen times). God isn't a helpmeet in the watered-down milquetoast way we've taught or understood that word within our churches, is he? No, our God is more than that: he's a strong helper, a warrior'.[10]

This is the word God chose to describe women – *ezer*, a word referring to military aid during battle and one that He simultaneously uses to describe Himself. I love that! We are meant to fight alongside our brothers in Christ – not in competition, not in front and not lagging behind – but united, working together to see His kingdom come, His will be done, on earth as it is in heaven. When we as women fully grasp our identity as *ezer kenegdo*, we can walk in our unique 'warrior strength'; a strength not dependent on physical muscle or a controlling need to prove our worth, but rather a character of peace and a stature of freedom. Walking in step with the incredible *ezer kenegdo* women before us – Mary, Deborah, Ruth, the Samaritan woman, Elizabeth, the 'sinful woman' at Jesus' feet, Anna, and a multitude of others – we never need to apologise for boldly living as strong women of God… because that is our heritage.

Dangerous distractions

While listening to a podcast recently, I heard the presenter say, 'The definition of doubt and double-mindedness is distraction.'[11] I had never heard it put that way before, but I like that description. Distraction is dangerous – and sneaky. It often isn't recognised until the deed is done and we are halfway down the detour route. We get distracted from the truth, our purpose or God's promises, and it immediately leads us towards a sea of uncertainty, questioning God's intentions and, eventually, our own identity. Recognition may not eliminate distractions, but it can help us respond appropriately, because one never knows when distraction might appear.

As I write, I am on sabbatical in America finishing this book at my parents' house. The computer is in the main living area, so anybody awake will either be sitting in or walking through that space on a regular basis. In light of this, I intentionally woke at 4:50 this morning to write in solitude. As it happened, my father had woken at 4:30 for an early morning coffee. Putting on my 'big girl attitude', I sat down quietly to start writing but before I could begin, he gently interrupted by asking me a question about an app on his smartphone. He had every right to be awake and there was nothing wrong with him asking for some help; the morning was simply not going according to my plan. *Deep breath. Respond in peace. Help him with the phone.* Laying down my frustration, I returned my attention to the computer, and picked up from where I had left off the night before... which was the first line of this section. Smiling, I remembered that wherever God is at work creating something wonderful, distraction will always be present, seeking to destroy. The more aware we are of this, the better we

'wherever God is at work creating... distraction will always be present, seeking to destroy'

can recognise its presence – responding with grace, wisdom and self-control rather than frustration.

As soon as God created humans in His own image, the enemy intentionally targeted that very identity by distracting Eve from the truth, planting seeds of doubt in her mind. 'Did God actually say...?' (Gen. 3:1) was the subtle, yet deadly, question presented to her. It only took him four more verses to seal their deaths, by suggesting her identity could be equal with that of her Creator (v5). Taking the bait (with Adam standing nearby, mute and motionless), Eve chose to believe the lie – birthing spiritual death. She was meant to walk equally alongside Adam, but instead she sought to establish – through naive deception – an equality with God. This choice shattered the very identity she sought after, resulting in loss of relationship with God as Father – a gulf between the Creator and His creation that lasted for generations. Through Christ our true identity is restored, yet the enemy remains equally vigilant today, causing distractions to keep us from fully embracing the truth.

I experienced a clear example of this many years ago living in London. I met a friend for coffee one afternoon, and as we were deep in conversation, a man approached. He was speaking gibberish and seemed to have some mental health issues. Showing us leaflets of random places and continuing to talk gibberish in a very quiet tone, we could not decipher what he was saying and it quickly went from bad to worse. Our apologies for not being able to understand him were met with frustration, as he grabbed his leaflets and left out of apparent exasperation. We felt awkward, but could not see any management staff to help, so we watched him leave, feeling terrible for failing to understand or help him. We soon became engrossed in our conversation again until my friend suddenly exclaimed, 'My phone!' The man who'd approached us was not confused, nor was he mentally ill – he was a scammer. He had slyly placed the leaflets on top of her phone while we were distracted trying to understand him, picking up her phone with the leaflets when he left, supposedly annoyed. In reality, he was elated because he had just scored a very expensive phone!

The enemy works in the same way. Speaking nonsense and untruths, he distracts us from our valuable possession (identity), stealing treasure, leaving us unaware of his schemes until it seems too late. He has stolen dreams, relationships, health and finances by spewing lies into the atmosphere, bringing confusion about the truth and diverting us from holding on to what is rightfully ours.

The Bible makes our identity clear:

'For we are his workmanship, created in Christ Jesus for good works, which God prepared beforehand, that we should walk in them.' (**Eph. 2:10**)

'Let us make man in our image…' (**Gen. 1:26***)*

'But he who is joined to the Lord becomes one spirit with him.'
(**1 Cor. 6:17**)

We have been made in the image of God, to do the works of God, by the Spirit of God. Identity is wrapped up in all three of these truths. Our identity is not what we do or how we look, but ultimately it is who we are; it is the core of our personhood – which is, quite simply, created in His image. And regardless of the distractive noise (lies) coming from the enemy, nothing can separate us from this identity as a child of the living God, adopted into His family as a daughter of the King (Eph. 1:5; 1 John 3:1).

Sarah Bessey beautifully sums up a confident woman by saying:

> *'Rest in your God-breathed worth. Stop holding your breath, hiding your gifts, ducking your head, dulling your roar, distracting your soul, stilling your hands, quieting your voice, and satiating your hunger with the lesser things of this world.'*[12]

In other words: be yourself. Walk that road of discovery and once you find that identity...

Live freely.

Laugh fully.

Love fiercely.

Power of Belief

Early rising

'Truly, I say to you, whoever says to this mountain, "Be taken up and thrown into the sea", and does not doubt in his heart, but believes that what he says will come to pass, it will be done for him. Therefore I tell you, whatever you ask in prayer, believe that you have received it, and it will be yours.' (**Mark 11:23–24**)

I love my early mornings. I realise that not everyone shares this joy of rising before dawn, but to me these are stolen moments with the Lord, held precious to my heart. I enjoy a still house and quiet streets as nature rests under her duvet of darkness. Those are the times I crawl out of bed – admittedly forcing myself at times (I'm not that holy!) – and curl up with my Bible and journal in my 'prayer chair', or alternatively go for a run while the streets are void of traffic and I am too tired to notice that I am exercising. Living in a variety of places has given me many diverse morning memories – from sunrise reflections on the English Channel to the bleating of sheep across a rolling, green pasture; from morning mist appearing over Regent's Park to the beauty of Buckingham Palace. One of my favourite memories is from living in Michigan, where we were often hit with large snowfalls overnight. An overnight blizzard had covered the trees and streets with a thick blanket of snow, and a palpable silence hung in the air as I stepped out for my morning run – in what felt like my own personal snow-globe.

The Gospels show that I am not the only one who loves an early-morning prayer time. Jesus was also partial to a good sunrise: 'And rising very early in the morning, while it was still dark, he departed and went out to a desolate place, and there he prayed' (Mark 1:35).

Personally, I think that sacred silence drew Jesus to arise early, or forego sleep altogether – not out of duty but out of choice. He relished mornings with His Father. Those times of interaction through prayer and worship may have rivalled His most precious moments with His friends; intentionally rising while it was still dark – undisturbed in intimacy, savouring the tranquillity. Prioritising time with His Father was shaped by necessity as well as desire. Jesus knew that He could do nothing apart from His Father and I believe those times of prayer allowed Him to commune with heaven, receiving instructions and guidance for future use. He needed to walk in wisdom and relationship at all times, remaining grounded in what He believed and who He knew, and this would only come through, uninterrupted quality time with His Father. If *Jesus* needed to walk with God daily, we can be certain that the same holds true for our lives.

Final authority

You may have heard the following: we are the average of the five people we spend the most time with. In other words, we become like those we know. For example, if the five closest people in our lives are full of negativity and fear, that will influence our atmosphere and impact our choices, hindering our capacity to thrive.

Alternatively, if they are full of faith and hope then our atmosphere grows stronger and our ability to thrive in faith increases. We cannot walk in one direction while the rest of our friends go in another; it will not work and will cause a tremendous amount of pain in the process. The Gospels give us insight into the ways of Jesus, including His interaction with others. There we observe Jesus' intentionality with His time and companions. In fact, there were times He only allowed a few to accompany Him (Mark 5:37; Matt. 17:1), leaving the other disciples behind. Clearly Jesus was not worried about pleasing men, nor was He concerned about equality within the ranks – He knew His identity and always walked in His authority.

When I finally chose to believe my identity in Christ, accepting it as fact over my circumstances, then my life radically changed for the better. I discovered that knowing your identity is wisdom, but walking in it is warfare. Many people know what they *should* believe, but their actions reveal a belief in something very different from the Word of God. We only fully know what we believe when we are forced to act upon that belief. For example, only when we have lost everything and need God as our provider will we know if that belief is head

'When I finally chose to believe my identity in Christ, accepting it as fact over my circumstances, then my life radically changed for the better'

knowledge or heart truth. It is the same with God as our healer, comforter etc. The same holds true in day-to-day events: we show our belief in a chair's quality by putting our weight on it. If it only has three legs and is wobbly, we likely will remain standing!

A scripture I used to quote regularly is Mark 9:24: 'I believe; help my unbelief!' I would emphasise 'help my unbelief', feeling quite humble and expecting the Father to swoop in, infusing me with the belief and courage necessary for my next steps. Recently I recognised the lack of faith in this (and the laziness) as I was not *choosing* to utilise the faith that I had already been given. Instead, I expected God to do all the work. One day I sensed the Lord showing me that my intense focus on unbelief was halting any attempt to actually believe. He said, 'If you focused more on believing, possibly you wouldn't struggle so much with unbelief?' Gulp. Guilty as charged. Therefore, over the next several months I spent hours with my Bible, researching and listening to many podcasts, clarifying what I believed and making that the final authority over what I saw. I chose to walk in what I knew to be true, regardless of my feelings or circumstantial evidence. In other words: belief outshone facts. It changed my life.

One of my most-quoted sayings is by Smith Wigglesworth (I am paraphrasing here): 'I am not moved by what I see. I am not moved by what I feel. I am moved by what I believe.'[13] What we believe must become greater than what we see in the mirror or feel on the inside. The Bible ought to have the last word in our lives and be our final authority, because that is where true identity is discovered and kingdom confidence can be birthed.

What shapes your belief system? Can you say that the Word of God has the final authority over what you see or how you feel? What would you need to change in order for that to be a true representation of your own life? As Jesus prioritised time with His Father, so must we if we want to walk in this level of believing. We cannot saturate ourselves with doubt and unbelief then hope to walk in victory and a strong, healthy, biblical confidence. Believing one thing but hoping for the opposite is both unrealistic and impossible. So how do we change the trajectory of our belief system? We begin by making alternative choices, seeking the help of the Holy Spirit and believing that as we take small steps, we will – over time – see undeniable life-changing results.

'We cannot saturate ourselves with doubt and unbelief then hope to walk in victory and a strong, healthy, biblical confidence'

What's on your mind?

Belief begins in our mind. What we think, we will eventually do.

'For as he thinks in his heart, so is he.' (**Prov. 23:7, NKJV**)

I cannot emphasise enough the importance of guarding our hearts and minds with all diligence (Prov. 4:23), because our meditations shape how we act and who we eventually become – to our benefit or to our detriment. Renowned Christian neuroscientist, Dr Carolyn Leaf, says that 95% of our thoughts are subconscious; in other words, merely 5% of the time are we consciously choosing our thoughts.[14] That is an amazing statistic! If we only influence our thoughts 5% of the time, we have given the enemy free reign to influence our lives 95% of the time, with no resistance from us. Walking in victory would be impossible with that kind of statistic, yet the majority of the time most people are unaware of who is controlling their thoughts. Dr Leaf writes the following:

'Thinking is the activity of the mind; and the mind is what the brain does. And it's in the thinking that good and bad choices are made. It's in our thinking that we choose to believe or not to believe the lies that our adversary, the devil, the father of lies, will present to us. It is his plan that we, as humans, passively receive his lies, think about them and – because of the concept of neuroplasticity – wire them into our brains. And, as we wire these lies into our biology, they negatively affect us spirit, soul and body… You are not able to control the events and circumstances of life or what other people think and choose. But you do have the power to choose what you believe and your reactions to the events and circumstances of life.'[15]

That last sentence is very important: we can intentionally choose our thoughts. There is no person and no demonic force that can forcibly decide our thoughts for us – we do that intentionally, or unintentionally, on our own.

But choosing takes effort, and therein lies the reason that many of us (myself included) struggle with thoughts that are not from the heart of heaven. It requires intentionality, awareness and repetition to change a negative mindset into one that mirrors biblical truths.

Quite frankly, it is much easier to accept whatever pops into our mind than to intentionally choose an alternative thought – that seems far too much effort! Yet not making the effort means we live at the whim of the enemy's tactics, paying the high price of forfeited freedom. (You can read more on this subject in my devotional book *Unstoppable*.)[16] Furthermore, if we are not conscious of the fact that we have a choice, we will allow the enemy and the world to dictate our atmosphere, with no resistance from us. That is not living on the kingdom level we have been created for. We are in this world, yet not of it and we are here to bring the rule of heaven to earth, not live under the control of earth until we see heaven. That choice is ours and I believe the effort is worth the freedom, for our own lives and for the lives of all young women in the generations following us.

'We are in this world, yet not of it and we are here to bring the rule of heaven to earth, not live under the control of earth until we see heaven'

I implore us to reject the lies of the enemy who whispers, 'It's too difficult. It would take too long. This is just how you're wired…' There are no excuses for remaining in negativity or self-pity – none. Philippians, considered to be the most joy-filled book of the Bible, was written by the apostle Paul while he sat in prison, surrounded by raw sewage and dank, dark, difficult conditions. Joy and positivity is a choice – always. The thoughts we choose to think become the words we speak over our lives; our words affect how we respond to life, and our responses develop the habits and behaviours by which we live. My thought life is not based on my circumstances, family, work environment or country of origin: it is based on a kingdom mentality that emulates Christ, honours all people and worships my Creator. The more we train our inside world to match this criteria, the greater our peace and the stronger our confidence – regardless of what is happening in our outside world. As Henry Ford's well-known saying goes: 'Whether you think you can, or you think you can't – you're right.' Paul clearly saturated his mind with joy-filled thoughts in order to write such an encouraging letter from the darkest of places. Philippians 4:8 (NIV) confirms and summarises this perfectly:

> *'Finally, brothers and sisters, whatever is true, whatever is noble, whatever is right, whatever is pure, whatever is lovely, whatever is admirable—if anything is excellent or praiseworthy—think about such things.'*

The Bible could not be clearer – living a victorious, joy-filled life means the eradication of any thinking that does not fit into the above criteria.

What amazed Jesus?

In Mark 6 and Luke 7 we see a fascinating compare-and-contrast scenario between a few individuals and Jesus. Mark 6:4–6 says:

> *'And Jesus said to them, "A prophet is not without honour, except in his home town and among his relatives and in his own household." And he could do no mighty work there, except that he laid his hands on a few sick people and healed them. And he marvelled because of their unbelief.'*

The background is that Jesus went home to Nazareth and began teaching in the synagogue. His words were filled with such wisdom that those who had known Him as a young boy were offended; how could one who once played with their sons be teaching them morality? Offence blocked their vision, draining the atmosphere of faith, thereby creating a scarcity of miracles. Offence is a ploy of the enemy, which is deeply dangerous when carried in the corridors of our hearts. It holds us hostage, allowing the jaws of bitterness to eat the fruit of peace. We may have a strong belief in the power of God to heal, but equally important to God is a heart of forgiveness.

> *'Truly, I say to you, whoever says to this mountain, "Be taken up and thrown into the sea", and does not doubt in his heart, but believes that what he says will come to pass, it will be done for him. Therefore I tell you, whatever you ask in prayer, believe that you have received it, and it will be yours. And whenever you stand praying, forgive, if you have anything against anyone, so that your Father also who is in heaven may forgive you your trespasses.'*
> (**Mark 11:23–25**)

Belief, faith, freedom and forgiveness are intrinsically linked together, dependent on each other to create our miracle. Forgiveness is a wonderful liberator: unforgiveness not only keeps us captive, but it is also like putting a stopper in our miracle. It is imperative that we let go of any unforgiveness our heart may be holding toward anyone. You can, right now, take it before the cross of Christ and release it to Him by faith. In doing so, we intentionally let the grace and peace of God minister to us, trusting Him to be our defender and judge, knowing that He sees all and *always* has our best future in mind. If helpful, here is a simple prayer you can use. (Remember that you don't have to feel like forgiving in order to forgive. Feelings may come later.)

Father, first I want to thank You for the forgiveness You have shown me in my own life. When I was undeserving, You loved me and sent Your son Jesus to die on a cross for my freedom. You have seen the hurt I have received at the hand of (insert person's name/s) and, by faith, I choose now to forgive them for the wrong done to me. (If you can, give specifics here.) I release them to You. By faith, I pray Your blessing over them and I take judgment out of my hands and give it to You instead. Thank You for loving me, restoring me and healing me. I believe You will 'restore the years the locusts have taken' and will mend my hurting heart – nothing missing, nothing broken. In Jesus' name I pray. Amen.

In contrast to the attitude of the people in Jesus' hometown, Luke 7:1–10 tells a story of great faith, found in a centurion soldier:

'After he had finished all his sayings in the hearing of the people, he entered Capernaum. Now a centurion had a servant who was sick and at the point of death, who was highly valued by him. When the centurion heard about Jesus, he sent to him elders of the Jews, asking him to come and heal his servant. And when they came to Jesus, they pleaded with him earnestly, saying, "He is worthy to have you do this for him, for he loves our nation, and he is the one who built us our synagogue." And Jesus went with them. When he was not far from the house, the centurion sent friends, saying

to him, "Lord, do not trouble yourself, for I am not worthy to have
you come under my roof. Therefore I did not presume to come to
you. But say the word, and let my servant be healed. For I too am
a man set under authority, with soldiers under me: and I say to one,
'Go', and he goes; and to another, 'Come', and he comes; and to my
servant, 'Do this', and he does it." When Jesus heard these things,
he marvelled at him, and turning to the crowd that followed him,
said, "I tell you, not even in Israel have I found such faith." And
when those who had been sent returned to the house, they found
the servant well.'

In this scene there was honour and respect shown to Jesus for His position of authority, by a man who understood authority. He was a Roman soldier, not a Jewish man, who had respect for a rabbi carrying an unspoken authority, clearly given by heaven. Walking in the presence of God allows the world to see what it may not understand – and surely cannot articulate. The centurion may not have quoted the Torah but he had a form of faith. It was this faith that amazed Jesus, and that He commended so highly.

Did you catch it? There are only two times in the Bible when it says Jesus was amazed – once by the lack of faith (Mark 6) and another time by the display of faith (Luke 7). The lack of faith was shown by those who should have known better and the exemplary faith was shown by a follower of Caesar, not of Christ.

Faith without demonstration is not faith at all (James 2:14–26). Only by acting on our faith do we reveal what our hearts believe. It is fitting to say we believe, but if our actions do not mirror our words, then those words may lose their authority and power. How are we practically demonstrating that we categorically believe

God is who He says He is and can do what He says He can do? Unshakeable confidence stands on faith, regardless of what lurks on the periphery. In his book *Shrewd*, author Rick Lawrence says it this way:

> *'Like the centurion, people who live under authority and exercise authority understand that faith is not about believing hard enough in something until you receive it. Faith, they know, is belief in the truth about who their Captain is, and therefore a certainty about His capabilities.'* [17]

God is capable. He is above every other name. Nothing is impossible for Him. He loves us. He is for us. His ways are beyond our ways. His mysteries are unfathomable. He is good. He always acts from a heart of love. He is with us right now and He is joy-filled at the thought of our future. Knowing all of that, I want Jesus to be amazed by me! If there is a choice between unbelief based on lack of evidence or genuine belief based on trust, kingdom confidence always chooses the pivotal key of belief. Which will you choose?

Destructive power of doubt

If belief is a key to walking in confidence, doubt is surely a padlock on the door to our freedom. The majority of my life was spent living in doubt, and I still find myself battling in this area. I doubted whether I was good enough, pretty enough, smart enough and strong enough. I lived under the weight of feeling like an imposter, convinced that one day someone would discover my ineptness and it would all be over. Promotions at work, ironically, increased my lack of confidence, causing me to strive harder and fear more. I have already alluded to wearing masks for a good portion of my growing up years and as I matured, they also matured – from false masks to good works. In my mind, if my performance could be 'good' enough, it would mean that *I* was good enough. Validation of my skills brought validation of my being. It was an exhausting and ultimately debilitating way to live. At the root of it all was lack of faith in my identity and doubt around my worth. I knew who the Bible declared me to be, yet the 'me in the mirror' held no resemblance… that I could see.

Doubt carries its own metaphorical backpack containing confusion, fear and failure – quashing faith and sabotaging opportunity. Remember Peter walking on the water? We may have heard the story so often the profundity is missed – Peter was literally walking on water. Not in it – *on* it! What a remarkable experience that only he and Jesus (I imagine) will ever share; yet in this passage we see doubt short-circuiting this amazing moment. I wonder how long he would have stayed on the water if he had not looked at the wind and waves and doubted? Perhaps Jesus would not have got in the boat, but instead continued strolling on the water, teaching Peter about the reality of God's authority over nature as they walked. Imagine the other disciples, wide-eyed as they watched this exchange, battling the wind as they attempted to sail where Peter had just stood.

Many of us spend too much of our lives in that place – allowing doubt to displace faith and consequently missing so much of the wonder we were created for. For me, there was no

'Eureka!' moment where I realised my worth and began walking in it. Rather, it happened over time and through many daily choices – choosing to believe God's Word and nature over my thoughts and feelings. I believe never being married has, surprisingly, helped in this area. There were days (weeks… OK, months) when I wallowed in my melancholy, angry at the turn of events in my life, tired of always being the bridesmaid and never the bride. But as years turned into decades, I discovered that I had a choice: either wallow in self-pity over my losses or worship the Father for my blessings. Not the least of these blessings is the opportunity my singleness has provided to do what I enjoy most:

> 'I discovered that I had a choice: either wallow in self-pity over my losses or worship the Father for my blessings'

I have far more time available to spend in private audience with my King than most married people have. This was not a decision based on feeling helpless or a resignation to a life of being alone: it was a choice to fully grasp what was in front of me at that moment, to trust and have faith that a good Father in heaven was producing in me, and through me, the best life possible.

Some will do this journey alone and others with a spouse or family, but regardless of who is in our world we must personally choose to discover our worth solely and completely in Christ. A spouse cannot give us self-worth; a role in the home – or out of the home – cannot truly validate us or bring us to a place of self-acceptance. Singleness is only part of my identity. My ultimate validation is found in Christ – and *His* definition is the one I have learned to trust.

The next chapter will revisit this area because doubt not only affects our belief but, if we are not careful, it can sabotage our faith. We need to guard against this if we want to walk in a healthy confidence, closing off doubt from any and all entryways into our spiritual lives. It genuinely is that important!

Part Two

IMMOVABLE
TRUTHS

Faith

Immovable

'For everyone who has been born of God overcomes the world. And this is the victory that has overcome the world—our faith. Who is it that overcomes the world except the one who believes that Jesus is the Son of God?' (**1 John 5:4–5**)

In my book *The Power of a Promise*[18] I share about the time my car rolled down a hill, without anyone in it, crashing through a neighbour's basement window. Thankfully they weren't home and nobody was injured! To this day I do not know what happened, as the night before I had parked it safely behind a barrier. To me, that is a great illustration of something immovable – moving. A parked car is simply not meant to willfully roll down a hill, taking up residence inside a window – so it's a picture indelibly printed on my mind!

While I champion flexibility and freedom, there are a few things in life that should always remain fixed – godly faith being one of these. Our Christian faith is meant to be unshakeable and cemented, regardless of the many storms battering us toward doubt or hesitation. Recently I was speaking in the West Country and I heard myself say: 'Doubt can pass through, but it should not push through.' In other words, doubt can pass through our minds, our worlds and our processing as a visitor, but pushing through to take up residence within our hearts, faith and expectations makes it a trespasser in the kingdom lifestyle. As the previous chapter strongly exhorted us – do *not* allow doubt a platform! It may state an opinion, but ultimately the voice of doubt must bow its knee to the voice of God, spoken through the written Word, which says we are to live by faith, trusting Him with all of our heart for a good outcome (Prov. 3:5–6; Rom. 8:28). It could be said this way: it is not wrong to have doubts, but it is wrong to entertain them and offer them food and accommodation for any duration of time. Please trust me on this, doubt is not a good companion; as with my car, it will move you in a direction you don't want to go, trapping you in a position you cannot seem to leave!

As thunderous waves remove a ship's stability, tossing it at whim, we give doubt the same power by granting it a foothold of opinion. Indecision is dangerous, both to our faith and to our desired outcomes. God will not override our free will; if we choose to doubt, the ramifications of that decision will affect our lives. God will not violate His Word because, unlike doubt, His Word is unshakeable, immovable and forever secure. Thankfully, in Christ, doubt is not our forever home.

Secure

There is no insecurity in the Godhead: the Father never gets upset if Jesus is worshipped and the Holy Spirit has no problem pointing us all to the Father. They are one. They are also the healthiest and most beautiful example of unity and kingdom

UNSHAKEABLE *Confidence*

identity we could aim to emulate. Questions never threaten God's
security as He thoroughly enjoys our dialogue, but (and this is
extremely important) at the end of the day, and after the issue has
been discussed, we have a decision to make: will we walk in faith
or won't we? How we answer that question will affect not only our
view of life, but how we live our lives and the resulting impact of
our lives upon our world.

We began this chapter with 1 John 5:4: 'For everyone who
has been born of God overcomes the world. And this is the victory
that has overcome the world—our faith.' God has given all of us a
measure of faith (Rom. 12:3) and He expects us to use it – not only
for salvation from hell, but to live out the complete freedom Christ
died to give us here on earth. Our faith literally overcomes the
world. In other words, the sin, sickness and destruction thrown
at us by the evil one are all overcome by the faith that we carry.
This faith helps us to live a victorious life and promises that same
triumphant living throughout eternity. What a gift! It is a faith
that says come hell or high water (literally), I will not be moved.

'immovable faith elicits unshakeable confidence'

I trust the Word of God, it is my final
authority, and I will never allow doubt
of the Word to override faith in a loving
God who sent His only Son to die for my
freedom. In other words: *immovable faith
elicits unshakeable confidence.*

It is this faith we carry as children of an unshakeable,
unchangeable God:

'Jesus Christ is the same yesterday and today and for ever.'
(**Heb. 13:8**)

'God said to Moses, "I AM WHO I AM." And he said: "Say this to the people of Israel, 'I AM has sent me to you.'"' (**Exod. 3:14**)

'Every good and every perfect gift is from above, coming down from the Father of lights with whom there is no variation or shadow due to change.' (**James 1:17**)

God does not change. He is, and always will be, God. And God is love: therefore He is, and always will be, love. The definition of love begins with 'Love is patient' (1 Cor. 13:4). In other words, God does not fly off the handle, make irrational judgments or act in haste – ever.

One of the best-known verses on faith is Hebrews 11:1: 'Now faith is the assurance of things hoped for, the conviction of things not seen.' Confidence and assurance are strong words, not ones easily swayed by the mood of the day or a change in season. If we want to walk in a healthy, strong confidence then we must remain in a healthy, strong faith-walk. We cannot be biblically confident and spiritually insecure. That would be like eating crisps all day then hoping to win a marathon – one will never produce the other.

I experienced this recently when outward circumstances pointed one direction and faith pointed another. It would have been easy to doubt the character and love of God, since in the natural He seemed fairly absent and indifferent to my urgent needs. One lunch with a friend changed everything. She lovingly, and with great compassion, challenged me to look at my faith-walk, examine the strength of my faith and make a decision: to either believe the scriptures within me or the facts of life surrounding me. I repented, passionately dived head first into the Bible, and have not looked back since. My faith advanced to a level I had only dreamed of and I am eager to see where it goes next. It is not without its challenges, as there are still a plethora of unanswered questions in my life, but my faith in an immovable God of love has been reestablished and reaffirmed. I *know* all will be well.

Perhaps you need to be reminded of God's love for you today? He sees where you are and hears your heart's cries. There are some things that have no explanation this side of heaven and I would not try to 'super-spiritualise' or simplify anything, but I *can* say that the love of God is without question and His power is without rival. He knows the end from the beginning and He always, *always* has our best future at heart. As a God of love, He can do nothing less. He owes me no explanation – He is God. And it is in that place where I choose to rest my faith and watch in wonder.

Father Abraham

Early in my Christian walk, I heard a preacher explain that Christians normally identify with one or two of the Bible characters in a special way, indicating the calling God has placed on their lives. Well, from the beginning my heart was toward Abraham and I loved to read and re-read his faith journey, impressed with his tenacity and encouraged by his humanity. He has been my most read Bible character and once I reach heaven, after spending a few thousand years gazing at Jesus, I may be tempted to join the queue of those wanting to chat with the 'father of faith' himself.

Abraham was given a promise at a time when dreaming was dead and retirement looked to be his only option. In the season of resting, God asked Abraham to believe for expansion.

'In the season of resting, God asked Abraham to believe for expansion'

Have you noticed that God rarely follows conventional wisdom? If practicality says go straight, then we can be fairly certain God will ask us to turn off to the left or right. He is intentionally and strategically working a master plan for our best life and for His glory. So, in his old age, childless Abraham is promised to become the father of many nations. In the natural, he did not have enough time. There were simply not enough years left to produce what God was asking of him, let alone the fact that two people are needed to produce a child his elderly wife's ovaries had long been redundant. We often forget Sarah had to carry and birth a child at the age of 90. Ninety! God must have supernaturally strengthened her muscles and bones to do what, in that day and age, a 19-year-old would be asked to do. It is quite extraordinary really.

For those reasons, and many more, I love how Romans 4:17–18 describes God's declaration over Abraham, and Abraham's belief in God's promise:

> *"I have made you the father of many nations"—in the presence of the God in whom he believed, who gives life to the dead and calls into existence the things that do not exist. In hope he believed against hope, that he should become the father of many nations, as he had been told, "So shall your offspring be."*

This refers to Genesis 15:5, where God showed Abram (whose name was later changed to Abraham, meaning father of many nations) the stars and told him that his offspring would be as they were – innumerable. Abram believed. He did not look at the facts, whine about his aching joints, lament the change in lifestyle or have an anxiety attack about what the neighbours might think – it simply says, 'Abram believed the Lord'.

Unshakeable confidence chooses to be faith-dependent in a self-reliant world. Abraham was not ignorant of the facts nor the impossibility of what God was proposing; he was expectant of the truth and of what faith could produce. Doubt is dangerous, but it is not the opposite of faith, as many believe. The opposite of faith is sight – and it can be far more dangerous than doubt. Issues arise when we allow what is seen (or at times, not seen) to distract us from the *un*seen reality of the Word of God in and over our lives. Living in victory means seeing with eyes of faith and allowing God's Word to have the last word.

> 'Unshakeable confidence chooses to be faith-dependent in a self-reliant world'

What do you see?

So, practically, what does it look like to have eyes of faith? 'So we fix our eyes not on what is seen, but on what is unseen, since what is seen is temporary, but what is unseen is eternal' (2 Cor. 4:18, NIV). Scripture beckons us to focus on the unseen over the seen, to trust in God, faith, the hosts of heaven and the Holy Spirit before we get distracted by our bank balance, the doctor, that relationship or our day-to-day difficulties. This is where our hope lies – in the unseen, never in the seen. I cannot put my hope in the government, a husband, friends, or even pastors, as they are all human and not designed to meet all my needs. God has already assured me that as I look to Him, He will meet all my needs according to His riches in glory (Phil. 4:19) and if He provides for the birds, surely I can trust Him to provide for me (Matt. 6:26).

One of the most obvious and tragic examples of this is found in Numbers 13. The Israelites have escaped 400 years of slavery and are poised to enter the Promised Land. The clue is in the title – *promised*. God has promised them this land… and He does not break His promises. Confirming the promise in verse 2, He says, 'Send men to spy out the land of Canaan, which I am giving to the people of Israel.' If God had sent them the signed deeds from heaven it could not have been clearer: God is giving them this land! It is a done deal. Finished. No begging or hoping it will work out, suppressing excitement in case of disappointment. No, this land was theirs for the taking.

And like all new homeowners, Moses was eager to gain a greater sense of what was soon (or so he thought) to be their future homestead. So he sent in some guys to spy out the new digs. They discovered fruit so enormous it took two people to carry it between them! This was not just land – this was prime, in-demand, top-grade real estate! The promises of God are always for our good, never for our ruin, bringing us hope and a brilliant future (Jer. 29:11) – exactly what He was providing for them in Canaan.

Unfortunately, ten of the 12 spies could not see beyond the giants of battles and barriers. Their sight brought fear; fear created despair; and despair produced hopelessness. Finally, hopelessness aborted their future dreams on the plains of a desert, where they concluded their days by wandering in circles for 40 years. To me, this story embodies the word tragedy. As a people they had suffered so much already, then finally the answer arrives, on a silver platter of sorts, and *still* the enemy blinded their eyes and handcuffed their faith – all because they chose human sight over divine promise. Without confidence our faith is limited, because faith by definition always resides *outside* our comfort zone, requiring a courage greater than our circumstances. Without faith we may miss some life-changing promises from heaven. God did not want the Israelites dying in the desert, but their unbelief could not be allowed to infect the faith required for the next season. They did not understand that their responsibility was simply to move forward on God's command – while God's responsibility was dislodging the enemy before them. Consequently only two men over 20 years of age – Joshua and Caleb – were able to enjoy a promise originally given to several million people.

'When we step out in faith, God moves forward in power'

When we step out in faith, God moves forward in power. It is a biblical truth seen throughout the Bible, yet many of us prefer moving our circumstances before releasing our faith. Unfortunately, it does not work that way! It never has and never will… otherwise it would not be faith.

Finally, let me add an extremely important truth (which we will revisit in the final chapter): a crucial key to victory is our perseverance. Without perseverance, faith will never fulfil its purpose in our lives. We must never quit. This is where many of us may falter, believing for a season but then getting distracted by the noise and busyness around us, causing us to begin sinking like Peter on the water. Never, never, *never* quit! Whatever is challenging your faith today, let the immovable truth of God's Word speak confidence into your heart, reminding you that He *always* has the last word.

Authenticity

Undisputed origin

'Blessed are those who hunger and thirst
for righteousness, for they shall be satisfied.'
(**Matt. 5:6**)

I remember visiting the Louvre several years ago and seeing the famous *Mona Lisa* painting for the first time. We had queued for what felt like hours to glimpse Leonardo da Vinci's masterpiece, expecting it to be awe-inspiring and (spoiler alert) larger than a postage stamp. While yes, it was larger than a sticker, it was much smaller than the showpiece I had imagined. I believe 'anti-climax' is a suitable phrase for that moment, as we crowded around trying to get near enough to see what was kept a respectable distance away. To an untrained and artistically uneducated person like me, I must admit – it seemed a slight waste of time and in hindsight I would have been happy looking at a poster instead! (Please don't write me a letter.)

But to the trained eye it was an elite tour de force deserving of adulation. The elite are unfazed by copies. Ironically, as much as society shouts about being original, much of the western world is tripping over itself to be politically correct and fit within ever-changing trends. Even Christians can get caught up in the nonsense, fearing we are not good enough because we don't measure up to Sister Super-Christian down the road.

One of the Oxford definitions of authenticity is:

'Of undisputed origin and not a copy.'[19]

I love that. Undisputed origin.

As Christians, our origin is an undisputed truth that nobody can steal. Each of us is an original and exclusive creation. There has never been, and never will be, a copy of you. In Genesis 1:26 God said, 'Let us make man in our image, after our likeness.' We have been made in the image of God Himself – it is as if He looked in the mirror, took a mental picture… and created you! *That* is the level of your worth and significance.

> 'Each of us is an original and exclusive creation. There has never been, and never will be, a copy of you'

Authenticity became very real to me on a blind date many years ago. This was back in 2006 when internet dating was still a bit of a taboo subject. Much to my chagrin I felt God leading me to sign up for six months, so after borrowing money from my parents (as if registering on the internet to find a date wasn't humiliating enough) I subscribed, and began the tedious process of vetting potential partners. I honestly believe a root canal procedure would have been more enjoyable. After a stream of unlikely partners (while some might find being the wife of a corn farmer in Iowa the perfect fit… I knew it wasn't my calling), a profile popped up belonging to a guy who appeared somewhat normal and loved Jesus. Winner. He was going to be in the area I lived, staying with his sister for a weekend, so it worked well for us to meet up. We had a nice time and after seeing him off at the train station I went home wondering how the story would unfold.

Within an hour my phone rang and it was him (this was

promising)... he began sharing that he enjoyed our time together (all looking good)... that he had come to the date confident that I would be great (oh, wow)... but that he never expected me to be amazing (is this really happening?)... and this had shown him that he wanted to go back to his ex-girlfriend.

(Stunned silence.)

He rabbited on after that, but I have absolutely no recollection of what he said, because all I heard was: 'Amazing isn't good enough.'

I had finally done it. I was amazing. And yet even amazing couldn't secure me a second date.

Shortly afterwards, the Lord revealed something I have never forgotten: it took amazing to show my date that he preferred authentic. You see, he already had an authentic relationship with his ex-girlfriend, he was simply too nervous to take the plunge and commit. But once he experienced amazing, he realised it didn't hold a candle to genuine. They got married and, last I heard, were very happy together.

The world raises the bar to amazing, but God sets the bar at authentic. The Lord prefers authentic over amazing and real over radical. I am not against church meetings done with excellence or incredible performances given to the glory of God – not at all. They can be awe-inspiring. But if we elevate amazing music over an authentic moment in the presence of God, then we have missed true spirituality and replaced it with the world's definition of success. Yes, it is possible to be simultaneously amazing *and* authentic, but authenticity must always take the lead.

'The world raises the bar to amazing, but God sets the bar at authentic'

The Jews expected that the promised Saviour would be a great king, all-powerful and filled with authority. Which is why a low-born baby did not capture their attention and a carpenter's son confused them – He was so… ordinary. But He was authentically ordinary – which made Him at the same time… amazing.

Uniquely righteous

Recently I was speaking at a church when they asked if I would say a ten-second encouragement to camera, which would be shown to an auditorium of teenage girls at a conference that week. Without any time to prepare I said something akin to the following: 'Girls! Do you realise you are each a unique creation? And because you are unique and there is literally nobody else like you, it is impossible for you to compare yourself to anyone else! By its very definition, unique means you are – unique. Therefore, you cannot be compared, or compare, because there is literally nothing else to compare with. It is impossible to compare what is actually… incomparable!' (Yep, I'm pretty sure I used the word compare 358 times within ten seconds.) Nevertheless, it's true!

And the same is true for those of us beyond the teenage years, when it comes to what I would term 'adult comparisons'. We compare parenting styles, financial status, career paths, spouse achievements, weight loss and yes… grey hair count. (Does anyone else deliberately breathe deeper to lower their stress levels, hoping to slow down the growth of grey hair? Just me then.) Comparing is quite simply a futile exercise at best and a damaging one at worst. Please stop trying to compare

'Comparing is quite simply a futile exercise at best and damaging one at worst'

what cannot be compared! If it means getting off social media for a while, do that. I have experienced seasons where I limited the social media feeds I perused, because I kept seeing others receiving opportunities I wanted or gaining blessings I had long prayed for.

Torturing ourselves with comparison is never life-giving and only opens the door to jealousy and judgment, so please nip it in the bud and go for a walk or read a book instead!

What I find fascinating is that to develop an authentic and unique identity, partnered with Christ-focused purpose, we must gain revelation of our right-standing before God. This is a truth I did not fully grasp for many years of my life, but one that is supremely important to walking out our confidence in the kingdom. Let's look at some scriptures relating to this:

'For our sake he made him to be sin who knew no sin, so that in him we might become the righteousness of God.' (**2 Cor. 5:21**)

'For if, because of one man's trespass, death reigned through that one man, much more will those who receive the abundance of grace and the free gift of righteousness reign in life through the one man Jesus Christ.' (**Rom. 5:17**)

'But if Christ is in you, although the body is dead because of sin, the Spirit is life because of righteousness.' (**Rom. 8:10**)

We *are* the righteousness of God in Christ Jesus. In other words, Christians are irrevocably in God's good books because of Jesus Christ, His death and His resurrection. Jesus has cleansed us from all sin, making us acceptable to a holy God without stain or blemish. This is the authentic life we have been created to live! And it was given to us through Christ's sacrifice, not earned through our striving. It is amazing to think that when a holy God looks at us, it is through the cross of Christ; He sees the blood of Jesus, not the depth of our depravity. Yes, we still sin, but upon heartfelt confession that sin has been cleansed and is no longer a barrier between us and God. Our spirit, which was dead in sin but came alive at salvation, is perfected in Christ and therefore we cannot be separated from the love of God – ever. What a Saviour we have!

For many years I knew that I was forgiven, but to claim that I was 'righteous' seemed a step too far. The ubiquitous sin in my heart (or my thoughts) kept me too ashamed to claim righteousness. And yet the Bible was very clear: 'righteous' is how God saw me. The gospel really is such good news

'Instead of fighting to walk victoriously, I chose to live victoriously – there is a big difference between those two'

that at times it can seem too good to be true! After reading the Scriptures and meditating on teachings about our right-standing in Christ, I finally accepted that I am righteous and therefore I am meant to live from victory, not endlessly trying to obtain victory. That truth changed my life. Instead of fighting to walk victoriously, I chose to live victoriously – there is a big difference between those two! After a while, I discovered there were many benefits we could have as righteous children of God; not the least of which is approaching the throne of grace with boldness, not needing to beg for God's attention or work for His favour. Further benefits include: flourishing and growing in grace in both youth and old age (Psa. 92:12–15), being entrusted with secrets by the Lord (Prov. 3:32), receiving blessings and favour (Psa. 5:12; Prov. 10:6) and rising again after failure (Prov. 24:16). That is a sample list of blessings we obtain through our relationship with Jesus Christ, but He will never force us to believe these truths. We must choose to believe them ourselves.

How high can you think?

For a moment, let's try to imagine Jesus with confidence issues. Can you envision Him asking His disciples how they thought the Sermon on the Mount had gone down with the people? Or apologising to the Pharisees for hurting their feelings when He called them 'whitewashed tombs'? Or praying over the five loaves of bread by shyly squeaking out, 'Father, if You want us to eat tonight, please would you consider multiplying this food?' It is ludicrous (and impiety!) to think Jesus would act that way, and completely out of character from what we see in the Bible. What if, instead of striving to reach an unattainable human perfection, we choose to believe that God sees us as He says He does – through the blood of Jesus, spiritually perfected and beautifully pure? It is from that perfected place that we are supposed to live our lives – no longer trying to achieve status, but living in the same peace and authority that Jesus carried. Jesus never viewed Himself as a victim; He knew His identity as the Son of Man and the Son of

God, and in that confidence, He lived out His everyday life.

One of the most beautiful examples of this is when a prostitute fell at His feet kissing them and weeping, yet Jesus never moved – unfazed by the opinions of onlookers, concerned only with the freedom of the one before Him (Luke 7:36–50). He says to Simon, a judgmental Pharisee, 'Do you see this woman?' It is one of my favourite phrases in the whole of the Bible. The beginning of that verse says Jesus 'turned toward the woman and said to Simon…' In other words, Jesus looked at the woman but spoke to the 'enemy'. He could not take His eyes off her, His love was so great. Imagine a couple in love, oblivious to the chatter around them in the restaurant because gazing into each other's eyes was all-consuming in that moment. That is how I see Jesus in this verse. The enemy was an intrusion, like a fly trying to distract a lover from his love – he needed to be swatted away. Why? Because Jesus saw her. *Truly* saw her. He saw her past, her pain, her hopes and her dreams. He saw her as a young girl running free, long before the world got hold of her, and He saw her as the woman He knew she could become.

Authentic love sees. And it sets free.

Imagine if you were Jesus and you died the gruesome death He died – to bring about complete freedom from all guilt, sin and shame for people. Then suppose that those you died for continued believing they were no good, intentionally criticising themselves, refusing to accept any type of approval or praise. Then to make matters worse, they thought this mindset pleased you! I don't know about you, but I would be slightly frustrated! If Jesus died to give us freedom, why choose bondage by putting on heavy chains called victim, low self-esteem, false humility and self-pity? (This is my list, you will have your own.) Let's replace low-thinking of self – so we don't offend God – with right-standing in Christ – so we honour His death. As we see in Jesus, walking authentically frees us from the need to prove (or protect) ourselves, allowing our attention to be focused elsewhere, helping others to walk free. One Greek definition of the word righteous is 'the state of him who is such as he ought to be'.[20] Don't you just love that?

To live as we were created to live, fully alive in perfect union with a perfect Saviour. No more. No less. No victim.

Purpose

Before you were born

'For we are God's [own] handiwork (His workmanship), recreated in Christ Jesus, [born anew] that we may do those good works which God predestined (planned beforehand) for us [taking paths which He prepared ahead of time], that we should walk in them [living the good life which He prearranged and made ready for us to live].' (Eph. 2:10, AMPC)

As a child I was consumed with a strong desire to 'change the world'. I had no idea how it would happen, but I endlessly dreamed of making an impact that would last well beyond my earthly years. My other distinct memory of childhood dreaming is me standing in my room 'preaching' to thousands of people, speaking with great power and authority… through my hairbrush. Ironically, at the time I was too shy to look at anyone, let alone hold a conversation, but nonetheless the dream was planted: I was born to communicate. As Psalm 139 says:

> 'For you created my inmost being; you knit me together in my mother's womb. I praise you because I am fearfully and

wonderfully made; your works are wonderful, I know that full well. My frame was not hidden from you when I was made in the secret place, when I was woven together in the depths of the earth. Your eyes saw my unformed body; all the days ordained for me were written in your book *before one of them came to be.'*
(Psa. 139: 13–16, NIV, emphasis mine)

Before you were formed, your purpose was imagined, and as it says in the opening scripture – this purpose includes living 'the good life'. Some children seem to be born with a specific desire to be a doctor, fly planes, take care of children or start a roadside lemonade business! We have innate purpose bottled up at a young age, resting like a rocket preparing for take-off, unleashing dreams from our hearts that will create a life God knows we will enjoy. Not everyone

'Before you were formed, your purpose was imagined'

has a desire to speak in front of thousands of people – in fact, for many that would be akin to torture! But for me that resembles the good life, predestined for me before I was even born. I believe Jesus understood His purpose from an early age, and was therefore content to remain behind, discussing religion with the teachers in the Temple courts (Luke 2:41–52) while His family journeyed home to Nazareth. He knew He was born to unsettle the settled. Growing older and stepping into ministry caused Him to become more vocal about His purpose, telling the disciples about His death and resurrection (Mark 9:31–32), aware that they would only come to understand His words after He had been raised from the dead.

Have you ever divulged your dreams to someone else, only to receive ridicule or misunderstanding in return? Sagacity, particularly when advising and encouraging young people, is critical if seeds of possibility are to firmly take root in their hearts. We must not be quick to dismiss youthful yearnings, as it often takes time (years even!) to discern our passions and discover where God is leading. The road may have necessary twists and turns, and because God works in seasons there may be some dreams that lie dormant for many years, or even decades. Being too quick to judge either our own or another's dream could damage or destroy what is actually meant to be germinating under the surface. Never abandon a dream unless God is clearly leading in another direction.

He is the author of new beginnings and a great resurrector of broken hearts. He alone knows the right season, the exact hour in which His wonderful plans for each of us will reach fulfilment. Our job is to trust that He has not left us or forsaken us. And as we trust, honour, worship and obey Him, we will find that He is clearly directing our paths (Prov. 3:5–6).

'He is the author of new beginnings and a great resurrector of broken hearts'

Prophetic author and speaker Doug Addison says: 'Changing the way you see yourself can empower you to walk in your greater calling.'[21] How do you currently view yourself? Are you 'just' a mum/housewife/small group leader/employee etc? Years ago, a friend challenged me about my perpetual use of that word 'just'. She showed me that inserting 'just' into a sentence automatically diminished whatever followed it; saying I am 'just a' (insert your own title here) somehow insinuates that it is a lesser role than perhaps a CEO or something else society often identifies as important or influential. If that sneaky little four-letter word pervades your vocabulary, I challenge you to intentionally remove it for 30 days. You will see your confidence grow as you allow your words to carry more weight and your opinions to hold greater value, by not diminishing them with this caveat. Initially this might be difficult, and if you are like me the temptation to blurt out a 'just' will be a gravitational pull comparable to the sun on planet earth – but don't relent! Believe me, this is not simply a nice exercise – it can be life defining! Our opinion is equally important to anyone else's opinion, so we need to learn to share it confidently and without excuse.

The power of opinion

Three of the most inauspicious words spoken in the Bible are found in Numbers 13:28: 'But the people...' Several chapters earlier, we saw an entire generation of Israelites miss out on their promised inheritance because they believed the lie that their fear-filled eyes saw in the present, instead of believing the truth that a faith-filled spirit would have seen for the future. The spies had just declared, 'We went into the land to which you sent us, and it does flow with milk and honey! Here is its fruit.' Then in the very next breath they blurt out, 'But the people...' and everything – *everything* – in their lives dramatically changes from that moment onward. The rest of the chapter reveals how Caleb silenced the people, trying to convince them that they were well able, but the spies had already infiltrated their minds with doubt. For Caleb it was as useless as trying to stop a moving train with his bare hands. As we have seen, doubt is a weed that grows quickly if not uprooted immediately, and I believe this weed grew in strength as they journeyed back to their awaiting families. They had plenty of time to talk among themselves as they snuck back to the desert. I imagine them discussing the strength of the Anek men, creating in their minds lost battles that had not yet happened, consequently feeling defeated before their bags hit the ground and their children hugged their necks. An entire generation was lost to the desert the moment they saw, and believed, that the dangers around them were stronger than the God who was for them.

The same happens in our lives. If we put greater trust, emphasis and belief in the opinions of people (regardless of their role in our lives) than in the opinion of God, we will lose what Christ gave His life for – our freedom. Listening online to Reinhard Bonnke's last African crusade I heard him declare that no pastor and no church can save us: Jesus Christ saved us and it is Him alone that we worship! We respect and honour our spiritual leaders, but we should never elevate their opinions above those of the Spirit or the Word of God. He is the one who saved us and He is the one who knows the plans He has for us.

When we put our worth and validation into the hands of another, we simultaneously give them control over our confidence. But once we know and believe what the Word of God says about us – that we are fearfully and wonderfully made for purposes beyond anything we could dream or imagine – then the negative, manipulative (or even well-meaning, but misguided) opinions of others hold less weight and ability to destroy what God is trying to create. This is nothing new: as we saw in Genesis, the enemy has been doing this since the beginning of time.

Remember where the enemy asked Eve, 'Did God really say…' (Gen. 3:1)? He was planting a seed of doubt in her mind:

'Do you really have the ability to hear God yourself, or did you misunderstand Him?' It is a ploy of the enemy to hold people hostage to the control of others, when God wants to teach us personally to hear His voice. We can all hear from God! Now, before I am misunderstood, let me emphasise that it is good and right that we listen to our spiritual leaders. I am not suggesting we walk with a rebellious or judgmental spirit, questioning everything that is said to us – absolutely not. What I am saying is that learning to know the voice of God is one of the most important and beautiful elements of our relationship with Him. Imagine if we had to go through our sister every time we wanted to know our dad's opinion – that would be tedious and ludicrous! A good sister would encourage us to approach the father ourselves.

In like manner, of course we can hear from God for one another, but even better is encouraging each believer to develop an intimate and beautiful dialogue with the Creator for themselves. He longs to speak with His children – all of them. Ask Him to give you a vision of who He created you to be. I would then encourage you to draw that picture, journal it, or find a picture that personifies that identity, and display it in a prominent place. Daily declare that identity over your future – and then enjoy the journey of becoming that person!

Speak up

Creation began with a word.

The Godhead was alive and moving, yet nothing visibly happened until God declared, 'Let there be light' (or more technically correct: 'Light: Be.'). At that moment, a historical line was drawn in the sand: before creation and after creation. The difference between them? Spoken words. God did not merely think what He wanted to see happen – He spoke it. And since we have been created in His image, so must we. The power of our words can never be underestimated. Sadly, I have often witnessed people (myself included) cursing their purpose through words of unbelief and insecurity, leading towards self-sabotage.

The Bible itself is *the* Word of God, spoken by the Holy Spirit through the prophets and apostles. Speaking this Word by faith releases a power into the atmosphere which carries life, healing and authority. We always have a choice of the words we say, so why not speak those we know carry power and the anointing of heaven?

> *'Death and life are in the power of the tongue, and those who love it will eat its fruits.'* (**Prov. 18:21**)

> *'I tell you, on the day of judgement people will give account for every careless word they speak, for by your words you will be justified, and by your words you will be condemned.'* (**Matt. 12:36–37**)

> *'Let no corrupting talk come out of your mouths, but only such as is good for building up, as fits the occasion, that it may give grace to those who hear.'* (**Eph. 4:29**)

As I said, we have control over our words; the words we choose will either bring life or death to our personal world and the wider world around us – there is no third option. Instead of it being a daunting prospect, embrace it as a daring prerogative. Christ has given us an enormous privilege as His ambassadors: the authority and responsibility to transform the culture around us to reflect the culture of heaven. We declare with our words that heaven's will is to be done on earth (Matt. 6:10) and confirm it by our actions. What an honour to carry this responsibility!

Have you ever been in the middle of 'one of those days', when suddenly something rises up on the inside (that something is the Spirit of God) and you declare, 'No! I do not receive this rubbish. My God loves me, He is for me, He is watching over me, and all things are working together for my good! Today, favour and honour find me, blessings chase me down and I have an expectation of a brilliant outcome!' Suddenly... everything changes! The room gets lighter, the atmosphere shifts and inside you feel more hope-filled. Why? Because you spoke truth and thereby created a different expectation around you and your environment. The enemy would love to keep us locked inside our minds all day, thinking and meditating on what is going wrong, or could go wrong, instead of looking for all that is right.

Worrying never brings improvement; it is an invisible chain controlled by the evil one, pulling our emotions here, there and everywhere. Some people find comfort in worry – yet to avoid admitting this, they call it prayer. I have been there. A mentor of mine used to say, 'Trust doesn't worry and worry doesn't trust.'

I had a choice to make – stop worrying or stop trusting. Admitting that made it easier to choose. One of the best ways to destroy worry at the root was to start filling my mouth (and mind) with something different – the Word of God. I began declaring Scripture in place of suspicion and believing the best instead of the worst. I also began dealing with things one moment at a time, continually declaring, 'All will be well' – and it has been. Romans 8:28 (NIV) states that 'in all things God works for the good of those who love him'. Either we believe that, or we don't. If we do, then we can trust that even the most horrendous situations in our lives, when placed in the hands of a loving Creator, will be turned around for something good and positive. This has been repeatedly tried and tested in my life and I can confirm – God is faithful. I am not 100% worry-free – like everything, it's a process and circumstances regularly tempt me to focus on my problems, forgetting my peace – but I am moving in and towards greater levels of trust. I have not only discovered greater peace, but I have found that my physical, emotional and mental health are all stronger as a result of this exercise. There simply is no substitute for the peace of God, which transcends all understanding, received as we release our worries into His ever-capable hands!

> 'do not be anxious about anything, but in everything by prayer and supplication with thanksgiving let your requests be made known to God. And the peace of God, which surpasses all understanding, will guard your hearts and your minds in Christ Jesus.'
> (**Phil. 4:6–7**)

Wait up

Many people are trying to be something they aren't, to get something they won't know how to keep, in order to live a life they don't know if they really want! That thought came out in a message recently as I was talking about a world filled with comparison and striving. In that environment it is easy to miss where we are, in search of where

> 'Many people are trying to be something they aren't, to get something they won't know how to keep, in order to live a life they don't know if they really want!'

we think we should be. The problem comes when our achievement is based solely on works, because then our own effort must maintain our position. Outwardly that sounds admirable. But if *God* positions us then He (and our obedience, not our works) will keep us there, and no enemy will be able to tear down what God desires to build up.

Do we have any 'middle children' out there? I have always felt in the middle. Born the middle child. In groups I was rarely the winner... yet rarely the loser. My grades were average. In school I associated with all, but aligned with none. I could speak up if necessary, but (as we know) was quite happy to be quiet. People said that I was attractive, but I was not a stunner... In other words, everything in my life seemed to point toward average. No matter how hard I tried, I could not get ahead to be in the front, leading the charge. Not that I wanted to be, mind you; I was too insecure for that. So the middle suited me well – in the middle, I could hide.

Some of you may be hiding from your purpose. The world around you seems to be moving ahead, yet you yourself feel stuck on the proverbial roundabout, finding no exit. Have you ever been running behind your siblings or friends and yelled, 'Wait up!' only to have them speed up? Yep, me too. I can still feel the rejection and hurt even now as I type this! Watching them saunter off into the distance, laughing at me, I felt abandoned and like nobody cared. In fact, I can remember several occasions where I simply stopped running. Gave up. Slowing down long enough to allow self-pity to catch up with me, so that we could throw a party together. (Self-pity loves a good party.) Joseph understood this feeling. He was thrown into a pit by his brothers and left for dead at the age of 17. You can imagine him saying, 'Guys, wait… come back… don't leave me in here!' He was in an impossible situation – those who should have had his back, intentionally threw him on it. But one of my favourite verses in this story is Genesis 37:25 (CEV): 'As Joseph's brothers sat down to eat, they looked up and saw a caravan of Ishmaelites coming from Gilead. Their camels were loaded with all kinds of spices that they were taking to Egypt.'

Sitting down, they looked up.

As hope sat down, help stood up. Whenever we feel hope has been lost, we can choose to look up. God will never leave us without an answer and – as in Joseph's case – often the answer is sent long before we know that we need it. Your answer is on its way. Quite possibly those who should have stood with you have instead abandoned you – sat down on the job, so to speak.

Look up.

Healthy confidence expects a good outcome. There have been a few times in my life over the past 20 years when I have felt in a pit, left for dead with no way out. And through each of those occasions I learnt to look up, expectantly, knowing that one day it would all change. It may take weeks, months or even years, but never stop believing that God has a (purpose-filled) miracle heading in your direction. Your caravan is coming.

> 'Healthy confidence expects a good outcome'

Part Three

DANGEROUS LIES

The Visible

Spot the lie

'Then Elisha prayed and said, "O LORD, please open his eyes that he may see." So the LORD opened the eyes of the young man, and he saw, and behold, the mountain was full of horses and chariots of fire all round Elisha.' (**2 Kings 6:17**)

In chapter two I mentioned my former senior pastor championing women at the boardroom table. Here is the rest of the story…

I was a youth associate at that time, one of four youth pastors overseeing the young people of the church. Every Tuesday the pastors and associates gathered in the boardroom with our senior pastor. We sat around a beautiful oak table discussing our various areas of church, with people throwing out opinions like confetti, all vying to get in the next word… all except me, of course. I sat there week after week, month after month… saying nothing. Terror can silence even the strongest of voices. Before you think unfavourably of my fellow pastors, they were some of the nicest people you could possibly meet. There was no sense of superiority by them or competition within the ranks (well, maybe a bit of healthy competition!) and my voice would surely have been welcome at the table, if I had chosen to use it. But fear muzzled me into silence, and one day I learned a valuable lesson as a result of it.

I don't remember the finer details, but the senior pastor was asking for our thoughts on resolving an issue. Immediately I thought of a solution, which seemed rather obvious to me, yet everyone else looked at a loss. Their silence convinced me of my absurdity – if this were a good idea then surely someone else would have mentioned it. The minutes ticked by and the longer we waited, the more I was convinced it was a stupid resolution. Eventually a few people threw out ideas, their voices devoid of confidence, while the entire time my heart was pounding because I desperately wanted to speak, but fear of looking stupid kept me silent. So I just sat there, leaning on my theatrical training, acting just as stumped as everyone else in the room.

Finally, after several minutes of weak suggestions, another female pastor said *exactly* what I had been thinking. The entire room looked at her in awe, expressed their unbelief at the obvious solution, and that's when our senior pastor said, 'And *that*, ladies and gentlemen, is why we have women in this room… thank you Dawn, that is the perfect solution.'

I could have cried. Sitting there motionless, I wanted to scream, 'Wait a minute – that was my idea five minutes ago!' But of course I couldn't say anything... because I hadn't said anything.

Once I recovered from my annoyance, I was struck by the fact that I had indeed had a brilliant thought, and though nobody would ever know I had it first, I knew. God wanted to show me that I had a voice

'God wanted to show me that I had a voice and that my opinion was valid'

and that my opinion was valid. He had given me the solution, yet I believed a lie over His voice, and my opportunity was lost to another woman. Lies will always steal opportunity, either from the one receiving the lie or the one speaking it.

Over the next few chapters we will explore some of the most prominent lies the enemy uses to hinder us from walking in healthy strength. He likes to get us focused on what we can see and hear in the physical, and the victim role we may consequently be tempted to play. His intention is never for our good and though his lies look like reality, they venture far from the truth.

I once heard a preacher say, 'We can know where God is wanting to bless us, by looking at where the enemy is attacking us.' The stronger the attack, the greater the potential blessing. I experienced this not long ago, when my finances were hit at a level I have never known. But through that tremendously challenging season the Lord set me free from a poverty spirit, giving me a revelation of some kingdom financial truths I had known but never fully understood. I remembered this principle early in the testing season, and became determined to come out of that season with victory. If you are experiencing persecution in an area, beware of the enemy distracting you into despair; instead, see it as the Lord putting a spotlight on the area He most wants to bless in your life, and then… walk in expectation of a great outcome!

Identifying a lie is the beginning of walking in truth. Growing up, the repetitive lie most prominent in my life often revolved around my opinion not being valid, or at least not likely accurate. This meant that the idea of using my voice terrified me as a child, and paralysed me as an adult. I lived my life assuming others knew more than me and if there was a disagreement of opinion, mine was probably wrong. This permitted me to be walked over, manipulated and controlled on a regular basis – even by Christians. Through them, I allowed the enemy to silence me. God had called me to be a voice sharing the good news to the nations, yet I could not even state my opinion in a boardroom in Midwest America. There are days I still stand amazed at how God has changed and moulded me. Steadily, over the years, as my confidence in the Lord grew, the confidence in myself increased. It was not an overnight transformation, nor an easy journey. I had years of mistakes, stepping out in fear and falling down in failure. But in the middle of it all there were some victories, and by never allowing fear to have the last word, my voice is slowly gaining strength. There are still situations where I feel afraid, where I back down or remain silent because of the company around me, but they are few and far between. Experiencing fear is not wrong, but handing fear control is never right.

'Experiencing fear is not wrong, but handing fear control is never right'

Under no circumstances should we allow the enemy to shame or embarrass us into silence. We have been given a voice to use for His glory and in a world filled with negativity and despair, I implore us to use our voice for good and to speak the truth in love. If we are a social media user, please consider before posting, liking or forwarding something – will this enhance the kingdom of God and is this a Christlike response? Negativity won't breed positive productivity and fear has never been God's method for attracting followers. This world is in dire need of wisdom, faith and hope. Will we be that answer?

The unseen

A few of my books have referenced my skydiving experience a few years ago – mainly because I cannot conceive a better personal example of what stepping out in faith looks like! Let's be honest – standing inside a plane 15,000 feet above the earth and *choosing* to open the door seems deranged. It reminds me of when David brought the Ark back to Jerusalem, dancing half-naked with all his might. His wife was embarrassed by his antics and thought that he had lost the plot, but David simply remarked, 'I will become even more undignified than this' (2 Sam. 6:22, NIV). Jumping out of a plane is not on the same spiritual level as worshipping wildly, but I imagine the adrenaline rush might be somewhat similar to the euphoria David felt at that moment. Standing at the edge of 'nothing but air', one quickly becomes aware of one's humanity, and even more aware of His greatness. Before I had time to elevate my fear to another level (if that was even possible), the instructor leaned me over the edge, the stunning green hills of England's north country in full view, and with the harsh wind haphazardly slapping my face, we jumped into the void... creating an experience I will never forget.

Physically, we are not created to stand in a vacuum; neither are we spiritually meant to see where we stand. Hebrews 11:1 says, 'Now faith is the *substance* of things hoped for, the evidence of things not seen' (NKJV, emphasis mine). As we saw a few chapters ago, faith becomes substance when weight is pressed upon it. Not seeing faith does not diminish its existence. I cannot see God right now, but I know beyond any doubt that He exists; if nothing else, because of the peace I have inside as I turn my thoughts and attention toward Him. Peace holds greater value to me than sight, because sight is based on natural reality while peace is based on *super*natural truth. Therein lies the difference between the seen and the unseen.

When the Israelites were stuck at the Red Sea, with an enraged army drawing fearfully close, they could see no way out. But in the unseen realm, God and His angelic army were already moving, preparing a miraculous escape route. Likewise, being caught far out at sea in the eye of a hurricane, the disciples could not envision making it safely to the shoreline. Yet Jesus, awakened from a peaceful sleep, calmed the angry swells by the unseen power waiting for His command. Finally, with her hope blinded by poverty, a widow was cooking one last meal for herself and her son before they prepared to die, when a prophet listening to an unseen God shared instructions that saved them from starvation and bought them a way out of poverty.

It is only natural to get caught up in what we see, because we live in a natural world and that is the way most people know how to live. But as the Bible says, we might live in the world, but we are not of the world (John 17:14–16). As such, we are not meant to elevate the world's laws above the Word of God. If God's Word says it is possible, then it *is* possible – regardless of what I see. Therefore, my bank account, health, relationships, business, family dynamics etc are all subject to change when I apply the Word of God to them. This is a powerful truth!

'If God's Word says it is possible, then it *is* possible – regardless of what I see'

The quickest way to strengthen our faith in the unseen is by regularly feeding on and walking in obedience to the Word of God. We need both of those – reading and obeying – in equal measure if we want to have a strong faith walk. The experience of my recent financial challenges actually cemented my belief in the fact that 'God is not a man that He should lie', as we saw in *Power of Belief*. One particular day of breakthrough came when I checked my current account to see a grand total of £1.19 staring back at me. I remember thinking I had a choice: laugh or cry. I chose laughter. Staring at that remarkably small number, through the largest smile I could muster under the circumstances, I began declaring God was my provider, all would be well, there was an open door of provision in front of me and all of my needs would be taken care of… in abundance! In other words, I chose to declare what I knew to be true in the spiritual rather than crying over what I saw in the natural. Writing this makes it appear easier than it felt at the time, but knowing my bank account would not even buy a small coffee put me in a disconcerting position: do I believe what I preach, or not? By choosing to believe in the unseen, I caused and (eventually) saw a drastic shift in the seen.

The apostle Paul intimates this:

'So we're not giving up. How could we! Even though on the outside it often looks like things are falling apart on us, on the inside, where God is making new life, not a day goes by without his unfolding grace. These hard times are small potatoes compared to the coming good times, the lavish celebration prepared for us. There's far more here than meets the eye. The things we see now are

here today, gone tomorrow. But the things we can't see now will last forever.' (**2 Cor. 4:16–18, *The Message***)

The NIV says it this way: 'So we fix our eyes not on what is seen, but on what is unseen, since what is seen is temporary, but what is unseen is eternal' (v18). The seen is always temporary when it comes to the world, but the unseen is eternal. We must diligently guard against the lie of the visible keeping us from the truth of the invisible. God's angelic army is watching over all of us, every moment. God is on His throne, Jesus is interceding for us and the Holy Spirit dwells within to guide our every step. Not to mention that we are surrounded by a crowd of witnesses in heaven cheering us on, waiting for our arrival! *That* is the kingdom of God and that is why we walk in kingdom authority and confidence, knowing that we are part of a much larger picture than our own limited worlds portray. Our lives are one thread in a beautiful tapestry of time, woven together by that which we will only fully understand after the visible has passed away. I encourage you to meditate on that truth today, allowing the unseen to override any seen battle you might currently be facing. He is with you. He is for you. And He will never leave you. Even if you cannot see Him at the moment… He is there.

A changeable God

In most play areas for children you will find a rope bridge lurking among the swings and roundabouts. Anyone who has experienced walking on one of these bridges will know that they breed anything other than trust! They are intentionally designed

UNSHAKEABLE *Confidence*

to sway from side to side, making it difficult to cross, providing very little sense of security. Sadly for some Christians, this is a depiction of their relationship with God. It leaves one feeling insecure, frail, lacking in trust and like the bottom could fall out at any moment. We will never walk in confidence or boldness if that is how we view our spiritual lives, let alone our Father in heaven. Through my own seasons of insecurity, I have learned that a 'moveable' God will always threaten my sense of faith and confidence. If my trust in Him shifts with every tough day or disappointing piece of news, then my foundations in God are not deep enough or strong enough to withstand a storm. Children need the security of knowing that no matter what they say or do, their parents are there to support them. If that security is absent, it can have a devastating effect on both their emotional health and their ability to trust (other humans or God) as they enter adulthood. It is that security, especially in the early development years, which shapes a child for life. If the child is unsure whether a parent will be happy or sad, present or preoccupied, then they will likely believe a lie – that God, too, is unpredictable – and they will walk into adulthood with a debilitating insecurity only Christ can heal.

One of the most prominent lies of the enemy is that our lives are a reflection of God's feelings towards us at that moment. In other words, if my world is going well, then God is pleased with me; if I am facing a challenge, then God is angry… or at the very least, disappointed.

'One of the most prominent lies... is that our lives are a reflection of God's feelings towards us'

96

This is simply not true. I can testify that every challenging season in my life has produced a greater character-building, faith-enhancing, God-empowering upgrade, which propelled me into my next season – without fail. I would never *desire* these seasons, but I have seen the power of God take my weakness and turn it into strength over and over again. There was one season I believed and declared a particular scripture for a year and a half before seeing the promise take shape and a door begin to open.

> 'I can testify that every challenging season in my life has produced a greater character-building, faith-enhancing, God-empowering upgrade, which propelled me into my next season'

Up until that point, everything in the natural seemed to mock me and scream that it was impossible. It looked as if nothing – *nothing* – was happening. Not only did it look hopeless, but it felt deeply hopeless. In reality though, hope was resting just around the corner, gaining strength, waiting for its cue. God was still on His throne, and He was not remotely worried, concerned or anxious about my situation. He was more concerned about my character than my bank balance or personal dreams; it was me who wondered how the rent would be paid and what constituted my next season. Yet as I focused on His lessons and my learning, every single bill, rent payment and meal was taken care of miraculously. I will never forget that season because it propelled me into another level of faith – a level I had desired yet simultaneously feared. God saw my heart and helped me get there, albeit not in the way I would have chosen! It forced my faith into action – would I trust God even when things around me were falling apart?

I am aware some of you have believed a particular scripture for much longer than 18 months – in some cases, for many years. There are promises I also have held to for many years (again, I speak much more about this subject in my book *The Power of a Promise*),[22] but the principle remains the same: God is not absent. We must guard against a victim mentality and an attitude of blame that tries to shift God from a position of strength to one of defence. At times we may want Him to defend why He has allowed something to happen, or not happen, in our lives and we can become frustrated if it seems He won't step up and engage in the fight. Because at the end of the day, that is what we want to do – fight the injustice we believe we are experiencing.

God does not need to defend Himself. Ever. He is God, I am not. End of story. The moment I think He has to approach my level and explain Himself, is the moment I have forgotten that the universe is held together by His power (Col. 1:17; Heb. 1:3) – the universe! By holding God hostage to my need for understanding, I limit my ability to grow in confidence: because if I only grow as far as I can understand, then my growth will be limited to what I can see, or at least what I can explain. Don't buy into the lie that what we see is all there is; the unseen is doing far more right now than we can see. Trust Him in the unknown.

The Vocal

Fear talking

'For the Spirit God gave us does not make us timid, but gives us power, love and self-discipline.' (**2 Tim. 1:7, NIV**)

It is impossible to watch the news, look at social media or walk past the local shops without fear staring you down with its beady little eyes. Our society feeds on it like ravens on a carcass. Without fear, most news channels would be on air for about two minutes, if that! Only a proactive stand will guard us from its toxic influence. Fear is not going away any time soon, and it is our responsibility to avert its influence over our world with its vile language and unhealthy input. We would never feed our children diseased meat and yet how many of us allow our families to watch and listen to fear-based programmes in schools, on our mobile phones or on TV? Being informed of the news is wise, but being controlled by it is foolish. The Bible says, 'For God has not given us a spirit of fear, but of power and of love and of a sound mind' (2 Tim. 1:7, NKJV). Fear-based living is not from heaven, and earth-based thinking should never lead our lives. Unshakeable kingdom confidence always chooses to speak life.

Where does fear speak the loudest in your life? Is it with your family, friendships, children, work, future, health, finances…?

There is no shortage of doorways through which fear can saunter to disrupt our focus and distract us from our purpose with its baggage of diseased thoughts, words and deeds. Anxiety and doubt can make even the bravest question their beliefs. Ask Peter what was happening as he walked on water, or what happened when a teenage girl questioned his involvement in Jesus' ministry. The normally brash and bold promptly became the weak and wimpy. God is looking for bravery, not bravado; and for the courageous, not the comfortable.

'God is looking for bravery, not bravado; and for the courageous, not the comfortable'

As women, I believe it is time for us to get our brave on! Let's rise up and 'fight like the girl' (to paraphrase Lisa Bevere)[23] He created us to be. I prefer to say it this way – we all have a bit of 'mama bear' in us. You have probably seen the videos of baby bear being approached by another animal, when mama bear suddenly comes bounding out of nowhere, running toward the attacker with a ferocity large enough to scare any encroaching enemy. One simply does not mess with mama bear! That same 'mama bear spirit' resides within every woman. I do not have children of my own, but I have kids in my life whom I love with such ferocity that I dare anyone to try and hurt them in my presence! Every woman innately knows that feeling – the desire to guard the innocent. It is inbred in us and is, I believe, one of our most beautiful traits. As Christian women we are strength embodied in grace.

This is how we must approach fear when it tries to invade our personal worlds, our loved ones, our relationships and our mindsets. We do not simply brush it aside; we get violent and refuse it access. The enemy is a legalist and if we tell him to go, he must obey. Just as we would not take time to negotiate with a bear, or feebly ask it to stop mauling our child, we cannot meekly approach the enemy of our souls muttering niceties and gentle requests. That is not his language and he will not respect it as ours. We must rise up on the inside, deciding and declaring that our lives, homes, families and communities are not up for grabs by one who does not carry authority on this earth. In both the Old and New Testament it declares, 'the earth is the Lord's, and everything in it' (Psa. 24:1; 1 Cor. 10:26 NIV). Satan is called the god of this world (2 Cor. 4:4) but that only shows his domain, not his dominance. God is still all-powerful and the earth is still His to govern (Psa. 22:28), which He partly does through us, His children and heirs, as we boldly declare His kingdom come and His will be done on earth as it is in heaven.

Before I am misunderstood, let me clarify that I am not suggesting we step into a spiritual level of authority we do not hold, trying to pull down spiritual powers we have no right to tackle. Pride came before Satan's fall and as we saw in *Power of Identity*, it will come before our own if we do not guard our hearts and walk with humility in our authority. Let me be clear: I am not telling the enemy what to do; I am coming into agreement with an all-powerful God who alone holds the ability to destroy evil and dethrone principalities. It is *always* God who does the work. We simply stand in agreement with His power, walking in the spiritual authority we read about in Matthew 16:18–19, and declaring the truth of God's Word in the name of Jesus (for Jesus *is* the Word!). Jesus died for our salvation, healing and freedom; and the gift of God is an overcoming life on earth and an eternal life in heaven!

Faith talking

I remember early in my Christian walk, I tested out this 'word stuff' in regards to a healing. I had pain in my knee, which had been there for years whenever I sat in a certain position, and I wanted to see if it would go away. I was not testing God from unbelief, but seeking Him in childlike faith. Feeling a tad bit foolish, I laid my hand upon my knee and spoke out loud that it be healed in Jesus' name. Much to my surprise (if I'm honest) I felt my kneecap shift underneath my hand and the pain immediately disappeared. I sat there dumbfounded. 'This stuff works!' was my first thought. It was a lesson I never forgot – our words carry power and God responds to faith.

'The power of our words and our faith is the creative power to bring heaven to earth'

By faith *and* words Jesus formed the earth, healed the sick, multiplied provision, calmed storms and defeated sin and death on behalf of all who would believe. Words cannot be separated from the miracles of God. Nowhere does it say that Jesus thought a miracle: it says He *spoke* and the miraculous happened. It would be much easier – safer – if we could think a miracle, then if nothing happened we would not be so embarrassed. But that, unfortunately, is not biblical. Faith acts and actions speak. The power of our words and our faith is the creative power to bring heaven to earth.

I believe that one of the reasons the enemy tries to silence our speech is that our words reveal our faith – and faith moves mountains (Mark 11:23–24). In fact, notice in these verses below how many times we see the command to 'speak' (emphasis mine):

'Truly, I say to you, whoever says *to this mountain, "Be taken up and thrown into the sea", and does not doubt in his heart, but believes that what he* says *will come to pass, it will be done for him. Therefore I tell you, whatever you* ask *in prayer, believe that you have received it, and it will be yours.'*

It is important to have faith and believe, but it is equally important to say what we want to see come to pass. When I made a decision to guard my mouth and speak faith instead of doubt, my world changed. That is not an exaggeration. I never realised how much the enemy had me focused on my mind, not my mouth. Words change atmospheres; I often see this when I preach. There can be an atmosphere of heaviness in the room because of all the challenges people are carrying, yet as worship is declared and faith is preached, the heaviness becomes lightness and despair becomes dancing. It is by far one of the favourite parts of ministering for me! I love seeing countenances change from morning to afternoon, or from the beginning of the message to the end. Recently, I was praying with someone who was grieving the death of a sibling. Although her sibling had died several years earlier, it was only as we prayed that she was able, for the first time, to cry over this deep sorrow. During the prayer I felt the Lord giving her a new name, which I spoke over her. She visibly began changing in front of my eyes, and within a few minutes, years of grief and a cloak of heaviness had been removed, making a new hope clearly visible – she literally glowed! To me, those sacred moments are like gold dust – precious and to be handled with great care.

Perhaps you have been disappointed, having stepped out in faith but without having received the result you desired?

This can understandably cause us to shrink back into doubt, allowing the enemy to easily steal any future breakthroughs. I will not attempt to explain unanswered prayer, as sometimes we must humble ourselves before a mighty God and bow to His wisdom above our understanding. I do, however, want to highlight the danger of never trying again. I am convinced that disappointment has destroyed many future breakthroughs. And trust me, I understand! Outlining the disappointments in my life would take many pages; grief, self-pity, hurt, doubt and anger took up residence in my heart for way too many years. I would periodically kick them out in great moments of faith or seasons where things were going well, but the slightest unmet expectation would open the door so they could march back in again, taking their well-worn seats at the table of my despair. Finally, I'd had enough. Refusing to spend the rest of my life see-sawing back and forth between joy and sorrow, I decided to immerse myself in the Word of God and find out what it really said about the faith and the blessing that Jesus died to give me. For me, it became not only faith-building, but doubt-destroying. Repeatedly reading the Scriptures in fullness and context made it impossible to miss the fact that Jesus died so that we could have a life overflowing with all the blessing and goodness the Father had promised Abraham, and even more so now that we are living under the new covenant.

Once I began speaking these scriptures out of my mouth, instead of the difficulty, doubt and despair I saw in front of me, everything began to change. Not instantly, but it *did* change. The first change I saw was within myself. My spirit felt stronger as I heard myself regularly speaking words of faith, trust, belief and joy. I found myself criticising less and desiring to encourage more.

I also began seeing blessings everywhere I looked – it is true that we find what we are looking for! And finally, after many weeks (months) of watching my words and denying negativity, sarcasm or doubt any air time in my vocabulary, I began seeing my circumstances change. That was a good day!

I will never be convinced otherwise – the spoken word of Scripture can impact earth by the anointed breath of heaven. It has power to heal, set free, create and alter what we see in front of us, outworking the plan of God in our lives. It is not magic dust that we carelessly scatter about, demanding that God do things our way. Some people have stood on the Scriptures for *30 years* for their miracles, and longer – perseverance is extremely important to victorious living. And, at the end of the day, if my breakthrough seems late in coming, I would rather be found in faith believing Jesus is who He says He is, than walking in doubt, allowing the enemy to usher in negativity and despair.

Finally, it is important to remember that declaring Scripture and believing for breakthrough is not meant only for our own glory or personal benefit. We have been blessed to be a blessing, but I cannot bless with what I do not have. It is impossible for me to give faith if I only carry doubt. Walking in healthy confidence includes walking in holy confidence. As we have seen, that comes from believing that the Bible has the final authority over our lives and that God's plans for us are always good and His Word is always true. Closing the door to the enemy's voice, regardless of our circumstances, opens the door to a stronger faith and a mindset based on truth, not facts. And I would suggest that is something to shout about!

'It is impossible for me to give faith if I only carry doubt'

Friends talking

As I mentioned earlier, it is vitally important to carefully choose who we surround ourselves with, because they will ultimately speak life or death into our worlds. Just as the enemy, and our own words, can produce damaging lies, the words of those closest to us can knowingly, or unknowingly, cause damage. Recently I did a radio interview for Premier Radio. Maria, the host, asked me how I decide who to share with when I face difficult times, including when I have been hurt by others. It was an excellent question and one I had not prepared for, but instantly the word *honour* came to mind. Before taking someone into my confidence, I want to know that they will maintain honour even over those who had hurt me. We honour people because *we* are honourable and we walk in honour to God, even if they do not. (Danny Silk has an excellent book addressing this called *Culture of Honor*.)[24] Honour does not mean we have to share everything with (or hide everything from) everyone – neither one is wisdom. What it means is that when we do share, it is done with honour – honour for ourselves, for our confidantes and even for our enemies – because honouring precedes being honoured.

There may be people surrounding us who are not speaking life into our worlds. In fact, they may be the very cause of our present heartache. But this does not give us licence to speak negatively about them behind their backs. There are ways to share difficult things without shaming or bad-mouthing someone in the process. We are not meant to judge someone's heart (that is God's responsibility), but we can judge the fruit of their lives. And we can talk about the fruit that we see, though we should not guess (or gossip) at the motive behind the action. I believe this is vitally important because the enemy can grab hold of the words that we speak: just as God brings life through our words, the enemy can bring death through our words. Have you ever heard someone say repeatedly that they were sure they would catch the virus going round (or fail the test, get the divorce, miss the deadline etc) and… of course, they did! We cannot repeatedly say one thing and expect to receive another – that does not make sense naturally or spiritually!

If we want to prevent lies from infiltrating our confidence, then speech has a powerful role to play. Friends who speak life, believe the best, cheer us on, lovingly speak hard truths when we need it and encourage us with scriptures are ones to keep. We need to surround ourselves with these 'keepers'! I have experienced this in the last year through a life-changing encounter with a friend. I was in a challenging situation, unsure how to move forward. After doing all the preliminary niceties with this friend, I laid out the challenge and asked her what she thought I should do. I was not looking for her to solve the problem, but rather give some perspective. She boldly began speaking faith, sharing about her own struggle in this area and declaring what God had taught her years ago – explaining that she is still living in abundance as a result of her obedience in that season. She grabbed my Bible, pointing out specific scriptures, then she firmly but gently explained that it was my choice moving forward – and that she would love and support me regardless of what I chose. Listening to her, my faith was awakened from its bed of despair and I could literally feel doubt begin shaking in its boots. What had victory over my life for many years was about to see the sole of my metaphoric stiletto as I drop-kicked it back to hell where it belonged! Becoming serious about victory, I cancelled my TV licence and Netflix subscription, choosing instead to spend hours and hours listening to excellent faith-building teaching, reading the Word of God, softly playing Scripture all night on my phone, and filling my atmosphere with praise and thanksgiving. I began sowing seeds of generosity wherever I could and I told those closest to me that they could only speak words of life and faith into my world, otherwise I was not going to share any further details with them. This was not a time for doubt, appeasing the curious or being spiritually lethargic; I was in a battle for my faith and I needed a breakthrough, which only total immersion could give me. Aside from salvation it was the best decision I have ever made. Those friends and family who journeyed with me have become part of a miracle story, many seeing their own faith reach new heights as a result. *That* is the friendship group I want circling me on both the joy-filled and faith-challenging days, and that is the vocal kind of faith-friend I want to be for those in my world.

'This was not a time for doubt, appeasing the curious or being spiritually lethargic; I was in a battle for my faith and I needed a breakthrough, which only total immersion could give me'

Though most people will never know the details of my unseen battles, God has seen every choice fought for and every tear shed, abundantly rewarding each difficult decision with His grace and faithfulness. He will do the same for you.

The Victim

Unattractive

'When victimhood is the source of your empowerment, recovery is the enemy.'
James Macpherson[25]

A victim mindset is deeply unattractive. I have never met someone engrossed in self-pity who radiated beauty, yet I have seen cancer victims beaming with incredible grace, because God's divine peace was shining through their eyes. True beauty goes far deeper than what one sees; it begins in the very core of who we are. One of the greatest lies holding women hostage today is that their beauty is defined by their success – success in marriage, children, business or body image. True beauty is never attached to what we do; it is cultivated in who we are. And while we can work at improving those other areas, none of them will make us beautiful – only the Spirit of God and walking in the fruit of the Spirit can do that.

'A victim mindset is deeply unattractive'

We are bombarded every day through advertisements, social media, films, magazines and the news with the message (lie!) that beauty is skin deep, that there is something deeply flawed in us, and that we therefore need to buy this product or do this diet to bring us one step nearer to that elusive standard we are hoping to meet. It is a lie cleverly packaged over the years and even though we may be aware of it, we still struggle to ignore it. There is nothing wrong with endeavouring to change our look or feel better about the way that we look, but making that the goal pushes aside the truth that God loves us as we are right now, regardless of dress size or scales reading.

Some of you may have every 'right' to feel like a victim. Perhaps there have been violations that have exceeded the physical, reaching the emotional – cutting deeper than anyone knows. It may have been at the hands of an abuser you did not know or a family member you did. Recently there has been a social media campaign with the hashtag #MeToo. Women from all spheres of life have been displaying it on their social media outlets, showing that they too have been victims of sexual abuse or harassment. There have been hundreds of thousands of women boldly stepping forward, and many more who did not feel the need, or the ability, to share that they too were part of this 'not so elite' club.

Abuse is not only sexual – it can adopt many forms. (If this hits any triggers in you when reading this section, please take good self-care and find someone appropriate to share with before reading further.) I am not making light – at all – of what anyone has experienced and I realise that there are no easy answers to fix what has, many times, been quite severely damaged. This book is not designed to be an in-depth look at abuse or to outline detailed causes of low self-esteem, but rather to point us towards a Saviour who wants to assist in healing those deep and very painful wounds… a Saviour who is completely trustworthy.

God cannot lie

I will never forget one rather unpleasant experience I had as a teenager after my parents discovered (through our tattle-tale little brother, of course) that my sister and I had blatantly disobeyed them. They were clever in how they confronted us: hiding their knowledge of the incident for a few days, cementing our belief that we had got away with it, therefore not agreeing a cover story between us. Consequently, we were completely taken by surprise when, a few days later, they came into the room and separated us before we could confirm our 'facts', taking my sister out of the room to speak to her first.

I remember staying in the living room waiting for them to come back, wondering if my sister was going to lie or not (this is BC – 'before Christ' days!). We had talked about our story, but we had not concluded what the final story was actually going to be. Knowing my sister was by far the more rebellious one, I concluded that she would probably lie – so that is what I did. Knowing I was the far more amiable one, she assumed I would tell the truth – so that is what she did. (As an aside, for any young people reading this, please tell the truth. It makes it much easier to remember and far less painful in the long run!)

Lying is one thing God has never done and will never do, as it is impossible for Him to lie. It is not in His nature and He cannot and will not go against His nature. Speaking about Satan, John 8:44 says that 'When he lies, he speaks out of his own character, for he is a liar and the father of lies'. Our enemy is the one who lies – never God. Therefore the Word of God is true, regardless of what my circumstances might show. The moment we begin doubting God's Word or His nature we have opened the door, allowing the enemy to saunter in and begin calling the shots with our soul, making it increasingly difficult for our faith to remain strong.

The challenge is that God *is* all-powerful… therefore, by definition, He *could* change the situation if He wanted to. But, that is not fully true. Yes, He is all-powerful, but He has also given us – and others – free will. He will never violate our free will, or the free will of another, and therefore decisions are made every day that are not of His doing or within His perfect plan. We tend to blame God when things go wrong and take the credit when things go right; it is human nature, but not at all scriptural.

If He did step in and fix everything, we would ultimately be robots at His bidding – without love or relationship holding us together. Love chooses. It sticks around, even when things are difficult; pain, trouble and disappointment cannot drive it away. Love continues to believe the best and not the worst, in spite of circumstances to the contrary. If we want that *from* God, then why is it challenging to do the same *for* God?

One of the most prolific lies of the enemy is 'God could fix this and He is choosing not to'. In other words, God is an absent parent figure, unfazed by our problems, appearing to be one way, but in reality being another. We all have a decision to make: God either tells the truth or He does not. And if I believe He tells the truth, then I have to believe it when things are going well *and* when they do not make any natural sense. My trust in God cannot fluctuate based on my circumstances, otherwise my trust is not ultimately trust – relying on results, not on relationship.

Be honest before God if you have doubts about His integrity

and love toward you – He knows it already, and remains deeply in love with you anyway.

Do you want to be made well?

Brené Brown says, 'We cannot selectively numb emotions, when we numb the painful emotions, we also numb the positive emotions.'[26] Personally, I have experienced abuse through a babysitter when I was about six years old. Details are not necessary, but needless to say the depth of the trauma caused me to block it out of my mind for many years. Only in my early twenties did the memories resurface, shedding light on patterns of behaviour and fears in my life that I never fully understood. I share a bit more detail in another book, but suffice to say my experience at a young age, and several more as a teenager, instilled a great fear of men and genuine disgust at myself. It took many, many years for the Lord to bring healing and freedom, so I understand the gentle process this takes and the fragility around the subject.

Despite what I have experienced, and having every 'right' to be angry and carry bitterness, I have realised that self-pity and unforgiveness are more damaging to me than to anybody else. That is the reason I want to address this upfront, because it is impossible to walk in healthy kingdom confidence while carrying a victim mindset. In John 5 we read about a man at the pool of Bethesda. As the Bible explains, this pool was an area where the sick would lie and when the waters of the pool

'it is impossible to walk in healthy kingdom confidence while carrying a victim mindset'

were stirred by an angel, the first to step into the water would receive their healing (vv3–5). The man in this story had lived with his condition for 38 years, seemingly unable to ever be first in the queue, regardless of his many years pool-side. I find it interesting that when Jesus approaches the man He does not address the condition, but rather the motivation. Jesus simply asks, 'Do you want to get well?' (v6, NIV) and the man replies, 'Sir, I have no one to help me into the pool when the water is stirred. While I am trying to get in, someone else goes down ahead of me' (v7, NIV). In other words, he avoids the question. He had spent so long focused on the problem, he never invested time believing for a solution.

Self-pity will do that. It likes to contain us in a pit of despair, shutting all windows of possibility and darkening any light of hope. I would often throw parties in my self-pity days, finding that self-pity had lots of other friends to invite, whether I wanted them to come or not: despair, depression, anger and hopelessness were some of my most frequent partygoers. Unfortunately this party was not one most healthy people would want to join. At times I had a few friends pull up chairs and sit for a while, but even they would tire eventually. I know for sure that the Lord was not keen on attending this party!

I am not intending any condemnation through my light-hearted reference to self-pity, because I believe we all struggle periodically in this area. Even the famous prophet Elijah battled self-pity and depression as we see in 1 Kings 19:4: 'he himself went a day's journey into the wilderness and came and sat down under a broom tree. And he asked that he might die, saying, "It is enough; now, O LORD, take away my life, for I am no better than my fathers."'

Jonah – one of the more reluctant prophets – told God, 'I'm so angry I wish I were dead' (Jonah 4:9, NIV). This was a little dramatic, given that all this anger was over a plant. Yep, a plant. Honestly, there is no end to the reasons we can feel sorry for ourselves!

Try to count the number of times David says in the psalms, 'How long, LORD, how long?' Psalm 6 is one I think we all can identify with: 'I am weary with my moaning; every night I flood my bed with tears; I drench my couch with my weeping. My eye wastes away because of grief; it grows weak because of all my foes' (vv6–7). Still, this was the guy who was renowned for his relationship with God, who said, 'I have found in David the son of Jesse a man after my heart, who will do all my will' (Acts 13:22).

So take courage, if you have struggled with self-pity, you are in good company… but I humbly suggest, there is a better way!

Moving on

'Why are you in despair, O my soul? And why are you disturbed within me? Hope in God, for I shall again praise Him, The help of my countenance and my God.' (**Psa. 43:5, NASB**)

Here we see one of the greatest antidotes to self-pity: thanksgiving and praise. There is tremendous power in thankfulness, far more than most of us realise. Not only thinking, but declaring, what we are thankful for can change our outlook, atmosphere and even the challenging circumstances around us. If your husband is the problem then begin thanking the Lord for

'There is tremendous power in thankfulness'

115

any positive trait you can think of about him; the same with your children, boss, colleague, neighbour or friend. There is always something good to be said about someone, regardless of the hurt they have caused. If you cannot see anything in the natural, then declare it by faith! This does not let the person off the hook, but it does allow you to begin walking in freedom. (I am not advocating you ignore abusive behaviour. This is never acceptable and should always be addressed appropriately. If you are experiencing abuse of any kind, or think you might be experiencing abuse, please speak with someone about this immediately.)

> *'Always be joyful. Always keep on praying. No matter what happens, always be thankful, for this is God's will for you who belong to Christ Jesus.'* (**1 Thess. 5:16–18, TLB**)

Always means always! There is always one area we know to be God's will – and that is thankfulness. Having a thankful heart brings health to our body (Prov. 17:22). Though it is no surprise, one recent study showed that grateful people had better heart rhythms and another reported that thankfulness can boost the immune system, actually increasing the disease-fighting cells in the body.[27] While we cannot control what has happened to us, we have complete control over our response today – and every day hereafter. A woman walking in healthy, kingdom confidence chooses joy, thanksgiving, forgiveness and grace. She does not allow herself to be walked-on or manipulated, nor does she feel the need to control others out of fear. Because she knows she is loved and totally accepted by her God, she can give love and acceptance to others, even when it hurts.

Donald Miller says, 'The most difficult lie I have ever contended with is this life is a story about me.'[28] That is such a brilliant quote. We are here to love and enjoy our lives, but our personal enjoyment should never be our finite goal. If it is, we will discover that we have lived a very narrow and self-centred life, missing out on the beauty of relationship and vulnerability, which ironically is where we find our dull edges sharpened and our sharp edges softened.

The dangerous lie is that we can do this life alone. That we can put up a wall keeping people outside, yet still live with kingdom confidence. We cannot. Whether someone has mistreated you verbally, abused you physically or spread damaging lies to hurt you emotionally, God always has the last word. It is not our responsibility to make someone pay for their mistakes, nor is it our burden to carry their sin. A healthy kingdom response to being mistreated is to *choose* to walk in forgiveness, receive healing, speak the truth in love and keep our hearts free from bitterness, anger and revenge. This cannot happen without the help of others and the grace of God, as seen in a widely recognised story...

> 'The dangerous lie is that we can do this life alone'

The evangelist

One of my favourite ladies in the Bible is found in John 4, where she is anonymously described as 'a Samaritan woman'. This woman had experienced difficult days, having had four previous marriages and currently living with an unmarried man. Many people assume she was a woman of ill repute, or at least a woman immune to the opinion of others. But my heart is soft toward her as I believe she experienced much abuse in her time and was never fully seen, or loved, for who she really was… until she met Jesus. He saw beyond her wall and into her purpose. Though she tried to deflect conversation away from her past, He methodically and beautifully performed heart surgery, all the while looking compassionately into her eyes and prophetically into her future.

The lie of victimhood is that we can never change, and will always carry with us the stains of our past. Thankfully, this is not heaven's definition. The Bible says we are a new creation (2 Cor. 5:17), that our sins have been washed white as snow (Isa. 1:18; 1 John 1:9) and that God has replaced the filth of our past with His own unending goodness (2 Cor. 5:21). That is an exceptional exchange! Yet how many of us look into the mirror, only to see our past still staring back at us? We try moving forward, but the pain snaps us backward.

For the Samaritan woman it took the love of Christ and truth of the gospel to set her free. After experiencing pure love, she began walking in the fullness of her identity: evangelist. John 4:28–30 says that she ran back toward the same people who, most likely, had shamed and shunned her, declaring, "'Come, see a man who told me all that I ever did. Can this be the Christ?" They went out of the town and were coming to him.'

In other words, within a few minutes of freedom she went from hiding to heralding and shame to shepherd. Her concern moved from protecting her own heart to setting free the hearts of others. Love will do that. It moves victim to victor and helps us see that our painful past can become priceless wisdom, used to help others discover their own road to victory.

Do not allow the enemy to keep you a victim when Christ has died to make you a victor. When we realise that our true identity is not bound up in our past, it frees us to begin seeking out who God's Word says we are, believing that over what we see in front of us. The journey will take time, and our identity will be revealed in layers; but with each godly decision, as we choose freedom over fear, we will find ourselves slowly becoming someone we only dreamed of being: healthy, strong and irresistibly confident.

'Do not allow the enemy to keep you a victim when Christ has died to make you a victor'

Part Four

BRILLIANT FUTURE

Design of Delay

One step at a time

'but those who hope in the LORD will renew their strength. They will soar on wings like eagles; they will run and not grow weary, they will walk and not be faint.' (Isa. 40:31, NIV)

'Are we there yet?'

I remember the exasperating sigh from my mother as she explained we had only been driving an hour and Grandma's house was still four hours away. That felt like an eternity to a ten-year-old. Grandma Baker's chocolate chip cookies were waiting on the other side – could this car not go any faster?!

As an adult I realise that in the scheme of things – and especially to an American – a five-hour drive is not actually a long journey, but to a child (or their parents) five hours can feel like five days. Time changes with perception and maturity, in the natural and in the spiritual. As we get older, our attention span grows and we need less and less outside stimulus to keep us from loitering at the borders of boredom. Though, as I type that, I wonder if an increase in social media and the overstimulation of today's technology have altered our attention span, causing us to revert back to the focus of a five-year-old? But I digress…

Regardless, it is a blinding lie of the enemy that constant

change is continual improvement; change is not necessarily bad, but it is also not always best. God is always moving, but He never changes. That is the paradox we must maintain in our own lives if we want to reside in His rhythms of grace. We move with Him, but as we read earlier, we are firmly fixed on an immovable foundation of faith, not altered by the seasons of life. It is that immovable faith which allows us to remain steadfast in the waiting season, when it seems we are not moving nearly as fast as we would like, the destination still hundreds of (metaphorical) miles away.

'change is not necessarily bad, but it is also not always best'

As it is in driving, so it is in life: the journey continues with one mile, one step, at a time. You could be sitting in a Concorde, flying at 1,350 miles per hour, and you will still only reach your destination one mile at a time. Yes, you might get there faster than those in a commercial jet but, bar a miracle of God, you will not get there instantaneously. When we remember this simple concept, then we can look at our journey toward confidence from the perspective of heaven's timelessness and not of earth's timing. We may not be where we want to be, but we are not where we used to be. And that in itself is worth celebrating.

Fake news

In my own walk with God, I have discovered that He often plants a seed in my heart months (or years) prior to its appearance. This is not a pattern special to me, as we see this throughout the Bible. Jesus was prophesied about, hundreds of years before His arrival; the birth of the Church was prophesied in Joel, hundreds of years before its occurrence; and, as we know, Jesus has prophesied His return – which we are still waiting for a few thousand years on and counting. God speaks a word, then time passes, and we wait… to see that word come to fruition. The phrase 'seedtime and harvest' could better be written 'Seed. Time. And harvest.' Time always holds space between the declaration and the destination. It is true in the natural, and it is equally true in the spiritual.

This is why we must not grow weary in doing good, and why we must not allow what we see to distract us from what He has said. The season of waiting is when the enemy does his most prolific work, using silence to try to throw us off course or discourage us from believing that things will ever change. He is a liar and the father of all lies, therefore *anything* he speaks is a lie or is shrouded in a lie. As we saw in the previous section, this is extremely important to remember as we seek to walk in greater confidence.

The phenomena of 'fake news' definitely did not start in America, or even in the political arena. As we have seen in the chapter on *Purpose*, it began in Genesis 3:1 when the snake asked, 'Did God really say…?' He took a shred of truth (there is always a shred of truth in fake news, which is why it's so dangerous), wrapped it up in a lie and… presto! Fake news was born. If you have ever thought or been told that there is not a good future ahead of you because of what has happened in your past, or the twists and turns of life in your present, that is fake news. Discard it as the rubbish it is! Possibly the dream looks different than you originally planned and maybe the lie holds a shred of truth, but my Bible says that God works all things together for good, and that is the *final* authority we choose to believe.

Another way to say this is: what may feel like delay is in fact development. God is outworking every detail for our good, according to the purposes He planned out for us before time began. We feel impatient because we operate within time, while He operates outside of it. It is like trusting a master painter, knowing that added time under his masterful hand will bring the work of art to the fullness of its beauty. Walking in unshakeable confidence means choosing to see our future through the eyes of faith, regardless of the passing of time. As we saw at the beginning, that is a choice only we can make.

> 'It is like trusting a master painter, knowing that added time under his masterful hand will bring the work of art to the fullness of its beauty'

Solidity

In Matthew 17 and Mark 8, Jesus tells His disciples that He will suffer and die, rising again after three days. This comes immediately after Peter's declaration that Jesus was 'the Christ' and before Peter's rebuke by Jesus – which came as a result of him audaciously rebuking Jesus first! Peter invariably had a good heart, but a wrong motive. He was more concerned with his reputation before man than his standing before God. Jesus knew that would be Peter's downfall if it was not intentionally dethroned and spiritually removed. Our greatest strengths will always be our greatest weaknesses if we do not allow the Holy Spirit to file down the sharp edges of our humanity.

In the passages above, Jesus was trying to explain in advance something they would only understand in reverse. Understanding this concept can help us navigate our own seasons of confusion. Another way to say it is this: God clarifies, then He solidifies. He clarifies what He plans to do, but then He solidifies in our hearts what needs to be done, in order to execute that purposed plan. The solidifying is where we often doubt the clarity we received. Just because we feel God has revealed His purpose for us, that does not mean it will happen automatically. There are many factors involved, not least our own journey of humility, allowing His timing to bring to pass that which His vision has revealed.

Previously I mentioned standing in my bedroom with a hairbrush, imagining myself speaking in front of thousands of people and inspiring them to draw nearer to a God who loved them. Earlier I failed to mention – I was not yet a Christian while I was doing this! But even so the seed was planted and to this day I can 'see' the crowds in my bedroom, more than 30 years later.

'My trust had been in the affirmation of people and not the authority of heaven'

At the age of 25, I was convinced that I was ready for the multitudes, and was confused when the doors didn't swing open before me. Two decades later, I keenly understand the deep work that was necessary in my own life, before God could entrust me with the lives of others. My trust had been in the affirmation of people and not the authority of heaven. As long as it remained so, I would forever struggle to freely speak what God asked me to share, basing my boldness on the shifting sands of opinion, rather than the leading of the Spirit.

What needs solidifying in your own life or character? Alongside several other deep works God did, He had to solidify my understanding that acceptance and approval came from Him first and foremost. He had clarified the call, but it took many more years to set the character, and He is still working on it! Though I moaned and complained throughout those years, I am forever grateful I was not given a wider platform prematurely. Many years ago I heard Joyce Meyer remark that God had told her: 'As many people as you can help, that is how many you can hurt.' And she emphasised the importance of leading well, carrying the influence of heaven with a measure of fear and trembling, knowing that with influence came responsibility. I have never forgotten those words, and though I have not navigated the journey perfectly, my heart's desire has always been for the name of Jesus to linger far longer than the name of Jen.

Our futures are brilliant and building a strong foundation of kingdom confidence is crucial, but we must never let that brilliance become worldly pride or think we have obtained success based on our own efforts. Delay reminds us that we are not in charge. That is a good reminder to have! As Peter needed the passing of time before he fully walked in his identity, so do we. And as we will see now, so did Joshua.

I see it

Let's revisit Joshua and Caleb one final time. I cannot imagine Joshua's frustration the day his fellow spies refused to see what God had promised. The Promised Land was so near… and yet so far. Hearing God say the land was theirs, and tasting the oversized fruit with his own lips… then having to wait *40 years* before taking the territory and enjoying the abundance –

all because of others' unbelief, not his own… well, I personally don't have the vocabulary to describe how he might have felt. God had clarified the vision, but the people's faithless response revealed that their collective character needed solidifying and their maturity needed to develop before their destiny could be fulfilled. Their lack of confidence, as we have seen a few times throughout this book, kept them from their destined purpose.

But Joshua and Caleb, being strong in purpose and identity, did not allow the setback to permanently frustrate them from an extraordinary future. We can read it here in Joshua 14:6–13:

'Then the people of Judah came to Joshua at Gilgal. And Caleb the son of Jephunneh the Kenizzite said to him, "You know what the LORD said to Moses the man of God in Kadesh-barnea concerning you and me. I was forty years old when Moses the servant of the LORD sent me from Kadesh-barnea to spy out the land, and I brought him word again as it was in my heart. But my brothers who went up with me made the heart of the people melt; yet I wholly followed the LORD my God. And Moses swore on that day, saying, 'Surely the land on which your foot has trodden shall be an inheritance for you and your children for ever, because you have wholly followed the LORD my God.' And now, behold, the LORD has kept me alive, just as he said, these forty-five years since the time that the LORD spoke this word to Moses, while Israel walked in the wilderness. And now, behold, I am this day eighty-five years old. I am still as strong today as I was in the day that Moses sent me; my strength now is as my strength was then, for war and for going and coming. So now give me this hill country of which the LORD spoke on that day, for you heard on that day

how the Anakim were there, with great fortified cities. It may be that the LORD will be with me, and I shall drive them out just as the LORD said."

Then Joshua blessed him, and he gave Hebron to Caleb the son of Jephunneh for an inheritance.'

Delay did not dampen Caleb's vision or Joshua's obedience. They were both ready to enter the Promised Land when the doors opened, even if it was 40 years later than expected. They had a deeper conviction, stronger confidence, greater wisdom and more seasoned fire in their bellies to take the land. Imagine the deep sense of joy and thankfulness they both must have felt on the day Joshua blessed Caleb. Standing there together, the remaining two from an entire generation who had forfeited their promise due to insecurity and unbelief. Yet they persevered, not allowing the surrounding negativity to crush their hope, waiting until the doors of favour opened on their behalf. As a result they now led the charge for the next generation, receiving every promise God had planned, not one missing or expired (Josh. 23:14). Joshua and Caleb persevered in faith to leave a legacy, not a following. It was never about them, but about the promises of God for their generation, and the generations to come.

Unshakeable confidence sees promise fulfilled, despite the bleating of a culture steeped in unbelief. Surrounded by the noise of competition, jealousy and judgment, we must stand strong for as long as it takes, believing God's Word and promises above all else. Confidence grows in this kingdom attitude, but capitulating to cultural pressure can methodically drain the air out of our spiritual tyres of faith, making us unable to complete the journey

'Surrounded by the noise of competition, jealousy and judgment, we must stand strong for as long as it takes, believing God's Word and promises above all else'

ahead. Where would you like to see your next breakthrough – in the physical, spiritual, mental or emotional? Ask the Lord for a vision of what victory in that area would look like, write out the vision (Hab. 2:2), share it with a trusted friend, find scriptures to support your goals and then believe for your upcoming victories. Regardless of how long it takes, refuse to give up. Caleb was a man of a different spirit (Num. 14:24) and he saw his promise come to pass. So will you.

Back Story Benefits

Our best story

'Blessed be the God and Father of our Lord Jesus Christ, who has blessed us in Christ with every spiritual blessing in the heavenly places' (**Eph. 1:3**)

Metro is a horse that paints. Yep, paints. He was a famous racehorse who retired out of injury and now produces paintings which earn money to help other injured racehorses.[29] It is quite the 'feel good' story and worth reading. What struck me when reading about Metro is that in the middle of his life everyone assumed his legacy would be racing – that was his gift, where he excelled and how he earned his owner's living. But as time has progressed, I daresay his legacy of painting may outweigh his glory from racing. It just goes to show that what we think is our full story, may only be the back story to our yet-unknown *best* story.

If his owner had allowed him to be put down, as some had suggested, then his story would have been cut short. And if, hypothetically speaking, Metro gained his self-worth from racing then his confidence would have been finished at the moment of retirement. I realise that a stallion doesn't normally battle self-esteem issues, but we can still gain powerful truths from this parable of sorts. First, life happens in seasons and a woman of confidence will embrace the season she is in, not pine after another. Spending our days looking to yesteryear, or dreaming of tomorrow, will never release the peace necessary to navigate today. Trust me, I've wasted many years trying! The sooner we adjust to our present season, seeking the nuggets of gold hidden in the darkest of places, the sooner we will see the hand of God navigating a beautiful picture of redemption, restoration and release in and through our lives.

'Spending our days looking to yesteryear, or dreaming of tomorrow, will never release the peace necessary to navigate today'

Each season also brings with it something required for the next. Metro's owner discovered the horse's talent because of the value placed on Metro as a horse of worth. His worth came from what he did, but ours comes from who we know. Jesus Christ has made us worthy, through His blood, and that worth means we will not be 'put out to pasture', unless we choose to go there. It may look like we have been left on the back field, but in the scheme of heaven our back field of difficulty can quickly become the battle field of victory. Just ask David. Summoned from the sheep fields to the frontline of battle, in order to deliver cheese – *after* he had been anointed king – could have been humiliating and frustrating. Instead, it was empowering and invigorating because David knew he was drawing nearer his destiny – regardless of how it happened.

Humility precedes honour (Prov. 18:12). And, as we read earlier, to fully walk in humility we must first know our identity.

Jesus was Saviour of the world, and He knew it, yet He worked as a carpenter and hung around an unremarkable neighbourhood for 30 years, waiting for His Father's timing. Even on the cross, in the most humiliating and degrading manner, He seemed a failure. We should not judge someone – including ourselves – by one, or even a few, season(s) of their lives. Redemption is more powerful than regret; and though there may be justice to pay in the natural (which is right), in the spiritual, it has already been paid. Judging Jesus on His season as the son of Mary and Joseph would show He was a good boy, but not a Saviour. Seeing Him with the disciples would show He is the Son of God, but not a Saviour. Even hanging naked and bloodied on the cross showed Him as a lover of mankind, but still not a Saviour. He became a Saviour when He ascended to heaven, keys in hand, victory declared. Jesus' most fruitful season surely would have appeared to be His three years of ministry, where miracles of healing and provision were in abundance, the dead were raised and the blind could now see. But that was His back story, not His full story.

Like Metro, Jesus had significant roles to play before the end of the book was read and realised. We must beware of venerating someone's back story, assuming it is their full story, until they have finished all their seasons. There is nothing wrong with celebration and honour – we should always be doing that – but if someone's worth and identity are attached to a season, then it can set them up for disappointment later in life. Perhaps you feel that your story has finished and due to life's circumstances you cannot see a better future ahead for you. If you are still breathing (which I'm assuming you are), then your story is not yet finished! Another chapter awaits, to enhance the fullness of your current life story.

Simeon and Anna were two elderly Jews whose full stories were only realised shortly before their home-going, when they prophesied the arrival of the Messiah (Luke 2:22–38). I believe they may have been misunderstood for many years, with people perhaps pitying them for their 'lot in life' – yet how many people

'what story may your life have yet to write?'

are able to say they prophesied the Messiah, even holding Him as an infant, before they passed into eternity, eventually meeting Him face-to-face as their Saviour? And so with you – what story may your life have yet to write?

Naturally confident

We have seen several times that vision matters and perception is pertinent to a healthy, promised outcome. Seeing ourselves healthy physically, spiritually, mentally and emotionally is important when surrounded by a society that feeds on flaws. Before I go further, let me reiterate that I am not criticising anyone who struggles in any of these areas, nor am I intending to condemn where life's circumstances have brought you. I am focusing on where we are going, from where we stand; not where we are standing, because of where we have been. There is a vast difference between those two and most people tend to see the latter and forget the former.

Let's get really practical. As I've mentioned, we cannot speak words of negativity over our lives and still expect to exude a healthy, kingdom confidence. For some of us the place to start is not spiritual, it is practical. It can be easy to super-spiritualise things and leave everything in the hands of God to 'do as He wishes', yet if we continue to treat our bodies harmfully we cannot expect God to bless them naturally. Eating poorly, smoking, drinking heavily, not exercising and turning to food for comfort are all decisions that will have a negative impact on how we look, which can have a knock-on effect on how we feel.

Where would you like to see some changes practically? The most important decision – without a doubt – is spiritual, as our inward health will often have a direct effect on our physical health. But our outward health and appearance are also important to walking in healthy confidence. So go for it and get a fun new haircut or a manicure if that's your thing! Perhaps you've been feeling the need to get more regular exercise, or cut out sugar for a time. A few years ago I did a three-week Daniel fast at the beginning of the year. For those unfamiliar with this, it is basically a fast from all foods except those Daniel might have eaten, as described in Daniel 1–10. (Confession time – I delved *deep* into the Hebrew and discovered that Daniel also ate Greek yoghurt and he loved posh coffee. I was pretty happy about that because I am genuinely not sure I would have survived the fast without those two key ingredients.)

The first week of the fast was not horrible, the second was excruciating (seriously, how many beans can one person eat in a week?) and the third was surprisingly freeing. In fact, I have never returned to my previous eating habits. I could not have predicted this change in my diet, but after those three weeks I no longer craved sugar (it was literally months before I had any cake). Instead I craved fruit and vegetables and would choose beans over meat most days. My skin also looked considerably healthier, I had more energy and I felt less lethargic and 'heavy' in general.

The few times I have needed to eat other foods, due to travel or speaking, I have felt much worse afterwards and quickly replaced my diet with fresh foods and water (plus posh coffee, of course).

This is not meant to be a boast from a moral high ground, or even to mask as a sales pitch to save the cows, but rather an example of a choice I did not exactly plan, bringing about a result I had always wanted. In other seasons I have made deliberate choices to exercise, watch my words, drink more water, read more books etc to bring about a change I wanted to see in my life. And through these I have learned that we have much more control over our futures than we realise. More often than not, it was lack of self-discipline that left me feeling less than myself, rather than negative circumstances.

Practically, what would you like to be different in your life? How could you see that happening? What is under your control and what is not?

As much as kingdom confidence has a spiritual root, which it does, there is also a natural side to walking it out. But the spiritual confidence brings the natural confidence, rather than the other way around, as society purports. All around us women are striving to look perfect and walk in confidence, but often from a place of self-will and not Spirit-empowerment. Once we put the Spirit at the centre, we have properly aligned ourselves to hear God's voice. We should never cultivate the natural over the spiritual, but the spiritual should always be alongside the natural in our choices.

Take some time to pray about which area the Spirit might be highlighting for your focus: investing in your prayer life, reflecting on certain scriptures, getting physically fit, taking greater care of your appearance, eating healthier, addressing an addiction, developing in knowledge, taking a risk... (add your own here). Then share that with a trusted friend – speaking it out loud is one of the most important steps toward change. Tell them what God is saying and then together discuss practical, small, first steps towards seeing this decision play out in the natural.

See-saw seasons

I remember as a kid enjoying the see-saw, trying to find a friend to join me on the other side. That part was tricky because you needed someone heavy enough to make it fun, but not so heavy that your feet never reached the ground! And oh, I can still painfully remember the feeling of a kid thinking it was hilarious to jump off at the last minute, sending me crashing to the ground, and walking away with a bruised backside. OK, maybe I didn't enjoy it so much.

Life can be like that see-saw – up one minute and down the next, month after month and year after year, until you wonder if getting off will ever happen. We are not meant to sit on a metaphorical see-saw our entire lives. There may be seasons, but as children do in traditional playgrounds, we too eventually leave the see-saw for more exciting ventures like roundabouts (perhaps not the best illustration), swings, monkey bars and slides. Why stick to one area when there is a plethora of others to explore?

'We are not meant to sit on a metaphorical see-saw our entire lives'

In Acts 3 we read about a man who had

lived a bit of a see-saw life for 38 years.

> *'Now a man who was lame from birth was being carried to the temple gate called Beautiful, where he was put every day to beg from those going into the temple courts'* (**Act 3:2, NIV**).

Daily he was brought in and laid down at a certain spot where he begged all day, until he was picked up and carried out in the evening, only to return the next day to do it all over again. That is truly the life of a see-saw – sat down, picked up, sat down, picked up, sat down… I imagine he never believed it could change and accepted that it was his lot in life. Surely Jesus would have walked by him to go into the Temple and yet this man wasn't healed (I believe he never asked Jesus for healing), which suggests to me that his vision never ventured further than his designated gate. Yet one conversation – one decision – changed everything.

> *'And Peter directed his gaze at him, as did John, and said, "Look at us." And he fixed his attention on them, expecting to receive something from them. But Peter said, "I have no silver and gold, but what I do have I give to you. In the name of Jesus Christ of Nazareth, rise up and walk!" And he took him by the right hand and raised him up, and immediately his feet and ankles were made strong. And leaping up he stood and began to walk, and entered the temple with them, walking and leaping and praising God.'* (**Acts 3:4–8**).

Through Peter and John he was offered a second chance, an encore of sorts, which carried with it a hope and a future. It did not happen automatically; the man had to offer his hand and work in partnership with Peter as he was raised up. Only then were his feet and ankles made strong, and he stepped into a new season, unveiling his full story, which had been quietly shrouded by his back story for many years. Perhaps it is time for you to jump off the metaphorical see-saw, to walk in a new identity, exploring all the adventure waiting for you in a fresh season of faith and confidence? What would that look like? What have you learned in your last season that prepares you to unveil a new strength and confidence in your next season? If a horse can paint, I humbly suggest you also have a new tomorrow hidden inside an unopened gift. Don't give up – your story is still being written.

Power of Perseverance

One more time

'Stand firm, and you will win life.'
(**Luke 21:19, NIV**)

'Try, try again…'

If I heard those words once from my father, I heard them a thousand times. It did not matter what the circumstance, how difficult the task or how stupendous the failure, my father had faith that there was a good future ahead, if I simply tried again. At 14 years of age I was annoyed when he said it; now in my forties I am appreciative of the legacy he passed on to us. He was right. There is always a tomorrow full of hope waiting for those who – intentionally – try again.

The importance of perseverance and not giving up cannot be overemphasised. Resisting the pressure to quit when attacks are fierce, and allowing grace to flow when mistakes are made, are vital to walking in healthy confidence. Whether you stand ready to risk rejection or are firmly planted behind a wall of protection, decide now that you will not quit until you reach the other side of healthy confidence. Stepping into the balance of identity and freedom must happen, as we saw at the beginning, through intentional choice. Believing that we are not indefinitely stuck in a particular pattern or mindset frees us to envision the possibility of a future aligned with the kingdom lifestyle Christ died to give us. Which way do you tend to swing – timid or tough? Is there a particular pattern you have seen repeated in your own life, confining you to a labyrinth of insecurity and fear?

As we saw with the Samaritan woman, Jesus is not concerned with the number of our failures, but rather He is focused on leading us towards a future filled with freedom. Let's meet another person who carried a hard exterior, living slightly detached from others, only to encounter radical change when he came face to face with Jesus:

> 'He entered Jericho and was passing through. And there was a man named Zacchaeus. He was a chief tax collector and was rich. And he was seeking to see who Jesus was, but on account of the crowd he could not, because he was small of stature. So he ran on ahead and climbed up into a sycamore tree to see him, for he was about to pass that way. And when Jesus came to the place, he looked up and said to him, "Zacchaeus, hurry and come down, for I must stay at your house today." So he hurried and came down and received him joyfully. And when they saw it, they all grumbled, "He has gone in to be the guest of a man who is a sinner." And Zacchaeus stood and said to the Lord, "Behold, Lord, half of my goods I give to the poor. And if I have defrauded anyone of anything, I restore it fourfold." And Jesus said to him, "Today salvation has come to this house, since he also is a son of Abraham. For the Son of Man came to seek and to save the lost."' (**Luke 19:1–10**)

Here is a man who had failed spiritually on a number of levels, garnering his wealth through the pain of others, yet Jesus ignored the crowd to change the one. It is interesting to note that Zacchaeus could not see Jesus through the crowds... yet, eventually, the crowds saw Jesus through Zacchaeus. We cannot spend time in the presence of God without being changed, and consequently affecting change in those around us.

If you feel you have failed Him, in whatever way, then today is the day to climb higher than the accusations and view Jesus from a new perspective. Intentionally position yourself to receive, allowing Him to meet with you, freely accepting the freedom He has to give… letting your changed behaviour be the testimony of a new tomorrow.

Time

Our relationship with the Lord is one area that nobody else can control – it is solely between us and Him. There are two key focuses that will strengthen our walk with Jesus and bring greater freedom: time and intention. If we do not spend time with the Lord and if we are not intentional in making different choices, then we will not see a change. It is as simple as that!

'There are two key focuses that will strengthen our walk with Jesus and bring greater freedom: time and intention'

As we approach this book's finishing line, I want to remind us once more of the power we all carry. I realise it may sound like a cliché, but there are no quick fixes to unshakeable confidence and our willful choices will make an enormous difference to a desired outcome. Nobody can make our choices, and nobody can remove our power of choice when it comes to seeking more of God – that is 100% within our realm of control. If we seek Him, we *will* find Him (Jer. 29:13). And if we want to grow in kingdom confidence, free from insecurity, detachment, fear or hardness of heart… we can.

How much time are we willing to invest into this journey? It's less about reading self-help books and attending seminars (neither of which are necessarily bad), and more about intentionally taking time to sit at the feet of Jesus, worshipping Him, studying His Word, receiving His love, getting to know Him as our best friend and greatest confidant. All healthy relationships need an investment of time, and our relationship with the Lord is no different. But it goes beyond daily devotions and Sunday services; it is cultivated in the moments walking down the road, standing in the grocery queue, waiting in traffic or washing the dishes. At those times as we talk to Him and listen to Him, we will come to know the still small voice at a deeper level.

Much has been written about Mary and Martha over the years and we can learn from both of their lives. There are seasons to be a Mary, sitting at the feet of Jesus, and other seasons to be a Martha, serving behind the scenes – or seasons to do both. Kingdom confidence always carries a bit of both. It knows that serving in humility comes from healthy strength and worshipping at His feet arises from holy surrender. We need

'There are seasons to be a Mary, sitting at the feet of Jesus, and other seasons to be a Martha, serving behind the scenes... Kingdom confidence always carries a bit of both'

both strength and surrender to walk in unshakeable confidence, showing the world through our actions that true meekness is a faith-carrying, sword-wielding, inner strength that never needs to promote itself. It simply *is*. By its very presence the atmosphere shifts, because the enemy knows that here is a woman strong in herself and her God. She will not speak idle words out of fear, but equally she will not be silent while injustice mocks the truth. This type of confidence only comes through time spent in His Word and around His nature.

Recitation or revelation

I believe there is a big difference between recitation and revelation.

Recitation is filled with repetition which, if we are not careful, will only go as far as our minds – never reaching our hearts. We can recite scriptures until the cows come home, but if it is done out of rote, then our behaviour will hardly be impacted. How many kids know that the rubbish needs to be taken out (because they have heard you say it a thousand times) yet it has not become a revelation in their hearts as to *why* it is important for it to take place? Therefore it may remain something they know, but not a habit they embrace.

I sounded like a broken record when I directed an anti-trafficking charity, telling the staff repeatedly, 'You must know the why behind the what, otherwise you will get burned out, quickly losing your vision and passion.' If we only do something because we think, or know, it is the right thing to do then we sell ourselves short of complete freedom in that area. I can know that it is right to eat my greens, but if I am only doing it for that reason, then it will rapidly become a burden, not a blessing. That may be the place you need to start and there is no shame in that. Repetition is not negative but (as we saw on the first page of the book) it is also not the full answer. Once I repeat the action of eating my greens for several days in a row (for example), and begin reading more about why it is important to eat healthily, I will begin feeling a positive change physically in my body, and then I am edging nearer the revelation of why I should eat greens – not out of compulsion, but now out of choice.

It is the same principle spiritually. We can recite scriptures regularly because we know it is the right thing to do, and we can read our Bible regularly to gain more knowledge, but if we do not receive revelation on why we are doing this, we will never advance from routine to relationship. And relationship is where identity – and kingdom confidence – are primarily cultivated.

Arguably the most famous scripture in the Bible, John 3:16 reveals this truth beautifully. Nicodemus, a leading Pharisee, knew the Scriptures better than most. Recitation was his middle name and he quite possibly could have recited the entire Old Testament. Did you catch that? The entire Old Testament! Yet he was missing out on the most basic principle of freedom, a relationship with Jesus Christ.

He saw that recitation taught him some truths (I wholly agree with memorising Scripture as an ongoing spiritual exercise) but it could not produce in him the greatest truth. Only revelation could do that, as seen by his final interaction with Jesus in John 19:38–40 (*The Message*):

> '*After all this, Joseph of Arimathea (he was a disciple of Jesus, but secretly, because he was intimidated by the Jews) petitioned Pilate to take the body of Jesus. Pilate gave permission. So Joseph came and took the body. Nicodemus, who had first come to Jesus at night, came now in broad daylight carrying a mixture of myrrh and aloes, about seventy-five pounds. They took Jesus' body and, following the Jewish burial custom, wrapped it in linen with the spices.*'

Nicodemus' progression from recitation to revelation is shown by his move from meeting Jesus at night to richly serving Him in the day. Revelation will do that. It frees us to be who we want to be, but are not sure how to be. It gives us courage to walk in our calling and it releases an inner strength which grows larger than the criticism or mocking around us.

Will you live from recitation or revelation in your next season?

Kingdom

Throughout this book I have intentionally, repeatedly, referred to kingdom confidence, because the way we view 'confidence' can change depending on our culture, upbringing and even spiritual home. But a kingdom confidence, one based on God's Word and by His Spirit, does not shift with the times – it remains steadfast regardless of the opinion of others. In Matthew 13:44 (TLB) we see the value of the kingdom: 'The Kingdom of Heaven is like a treasure a man discovered in a field. In his excitement, he sold everything he owned to get enough money to buy the field—and get the treasure, too!' It is a treasure worth pursuing and sacrificing for, having value that far outweighs anything the world has to offer. And so it is when it comes to kingdom confidence. Knowing who we are in the eyes of heaven is worth far more than the views of a magazine, social media post or

> 'Putting our trust in the King's perspective, will ultimately put truth into ours'

even the opinions of family and friends. Putting our trust in the King's perspective will ultimately put truth into ours.

Throughout our journey together, my prayer for you has been that you will discover the 'you' that God designed you to be, the 'you' you have always wanted to be. There will be a security unleashed on the inside and a peace unveiled on the outside. No longer will you walk ashamed, afraid or guarded, but instead you will walk with an inner calm and confidence that exudes the strength of a general and the peace of the gentle. I believe through knowing the keys, walking in the truths, identifying the lies and embracing your future – it *is* possible!

> 'But you are the ones chosen by God, chosen for the high calling of priestly work, chosen to be a holy people, God's instruments to do his work and speak out for him, to tell others of the night-and-day difference he made for you—from nothing to something, from rejected to accepted.' (**1 Pet. 2:9–10, *The Message***)

Father,

Thank You for journeying with us through this book. I pray now for the one reading this final prayer, that You would be very near to her, shining Your light of grace over her hopes, dreams, regrets, hurts, challenges and desires. Work together for good all that You have ordained, allowing her to shine in health and wholeness spiritually, physically, mentally and emotionally. Journey her toward her best story, written by heaven and lived on earth.

Bless her abundantly, I pray. Amen.

Author's Notes

We made it! I am so pleased you joined me on this journey toward unshakeable confidence and I pray you have been encouraged, challenged and blessed by our time together. I give God all the glory for how He has blessed my life and I have no greater desire than seeing others walking in victory with Him.

If you have never made Jesus the Lord of your life, or if you would like to rededicate your life to Him, please join me in praying the following prayer:

> **Dear God,**
>
> **I come to You in the name of Jesus. I admit that I have not trusted You to be my Saviour and have tried to live on my own terms. I ask You to forgive me of all my sins. The Bible says if I confess with my mouth that 'Jesus is Lord', and believe in my heart that God raised Him from the dead, I will be saved (Rom. 10:9). I believe with my heart and I confess with my mouth that Jesus is the Lord and Saviour of my life from this moment forward. Thank You for saving me!**
>
> **In Jesus' name, I pray. Amen.**

If you have prayed that prayer, I would love to celebrate with you! Please let me know by emailing your testimony to **jen@jenbaker.co.uk**. Also, please share with a trusted friend and find a strong Bible-teaching, Spirit-filled church to become part of, as we cannot do this journey alone.

Finally, I would love to stay in touch with you through social media. You can find me on Instagram, Facebook and Twitter here: @jenbakerinspire

Other books by Jen Baker:
— *Untangled* (Farnham: CWR, 2013)
— *Unlimited* (Farnham: CWR, 2014)
— *Unstoppable* (Farnham: CWR, 2018)
— *The Power of a Promise* (Milton Keynes: Authentic Media, 2018)

Endnotes

Please note: all online content accessed and correct at time of writing (December 2017).

[1] Brené Brown, *Daring Greatly* (New York: Penguin Group, 2012), p37

[2] Charles Spurgeon @spurgeonbooks, 'When a man admires himself he never adores God.' Instagram post: 04/08/2017

[3] @copelandnetwork, 'I will allow the Father to meet the needs of my soul, so that I can be free from the need to perform.' Instagram post: 09/11/ 2017

[4] Sarah Bessey, *Jesus Feminist* (London: Darton, Longman and Todd Ltd, 2013), (Kindle version)

[5] Englishman's Concordance, found at www.biblehub.com/hebrew/kenegdo

[6] Englishman's Concordance, found at www.biblehub.com/hebrew/ezer

[7] Carolyn Custis James, *Half the Church: Recapturing God's Global Vision for Women* (Grand Rapids, MI, USA: Zondervan, 2010), p154, cited by Sarah Bessey, *Jesus Feminist* (London: Darton, Longman and Todd Ltd, 2013), p77

[8] Strong's Concordance, found at www.biblehub.com/hebrew

[9] Victor Hamilton, cited by Carolyn Custis James, 'It's a Man's Prerogative to Change His Mind' *Christian History Institute*, blog posted on 26/01/2017, found at www.christianhistoryinstitute.org

[10] Sarah Bessey, *Jesus Feminist* (London: Darton, Longman and Todd Ltd, 2013), (Kindle version)

[11] Kellie Copeland, BVOV Audio Podcast: 09/11/ 2017

[12] Sarah Bessey, *Jesus Feminist* (London: Darton, Longman and Todd Ltd, 2013), (Kindle version)

[13] Smith Wigglesworth, *The Power of the Name*, found at www.smithwigglesworth.com

[14] Dr Caroline Leaf, *Switch on Your Brain*, found at www.renewingallthings.com

[15] Dr Caroline Leaf, *What Lies Are You Believing?*, found at www.drleaf.com

[16] Jen Baker, *Unstoppable* (Farnham: CWR, 2018)

[17] Rick Lawrence, *Shrewd* (Colorado Springs: David C. Cook, 2012), p254

[18] Jen Baker, *The Power of a Promise* (Milton Keynes: Authentic Media, 2018)

[19] English Oxford Living Dictionaries, found at www.en.oxforddictionaries.com/definition/authentic

[20] Strong's Concordance, found at www.biblehub.com/greek

[21] Doug Addison @dougtaddison, 'Changing the way you see yourself can empower you to walk in your greater calling.' Instagram post: 02/10/2017

[22] Jen Baker, *The Power of a Promise* (Milton Keynes: Authentic Media, 2018)

[23] Lisa Bevere, *Fight Like a Girl* (Boston: Little, Brown & Company, 2006)

[24] Danny Silk, *Culture of Honor: Sustaining A Supernatural Environment* (Shippensburg: Destiny Image Publishers, 2013)

[25] James Macpherson @jamesmacpherson, 'When victimhood is the source of your empowerment, recovery is the enemy.' Twitter post: 10/11/2017

[26] Brené Brown, *The Gifts of Imperfection: Let Go of Who You Think You're Supposed to Be and Embrace Who You Are* (Center City: Hazelden, 2010)

[27] Lauren Dunn, 'Be thankful: Science says gratitude is good for your health,' *Today*, blog posted 26/11/2015, 3.15pm

[28] Donald Miller, 'The most difficult lie I have ever contended with is this life is a story about me.' Found at www.goodreads.com

[29] Claire Bates, 'The horse that saved his own life by painting', BBC News: 01/05/2017

Inspiring
Women

Two ways to spend quality time with God

Inspiring Women Every Day

Written by women for women, these daily Bible reading notes offer insights that can be applied to your life every day. Discover more titles in the Inspiring Women range on our website.

Courses and Seminars

Our courses and seminars are designed for women of all ages and walks of life, creating opportunities to dig deeper into a relationship with God. Come and enjoy insightful teaching, worship and warm fellowship.

We can also bring some of our courses to your church or small group.

Find out more about all our resources and courses for women at
cwr.org.uk/inspiringwomen

More from Jen Baker

These 12-week devotional journals explore key themes such as identity, purpose and how to transform negative mindsets. Each journal includes scriptures and thought-provoking questions.

God is good.
He has good plans for you.

Fear and regrets can often hold us back. Learn how to overcome such challenges by exploring different 'Freedom from' themes and delve into a transformative time with God.
ISBN: 978-1-85345-917-7

God's love for us is limitless...

He wants us to live a life full of purpose, unrestricted by the things that try to lessen our true identity in Jesus.
ISBN: 978-1-78259-398-0

Learn how to think like the child of God that you are!

What we believe affects every area of our lives. So how can we meditate on God's Word until His truth becomes our belief?
ISBN: 978-1-78259-754-4

For more information, current prices and to order visit
cwr.org.uk/inspiringwomen

Courses and seminars

Waverley Abbey College

Publishing and media

Conference facilities

Transforming lives

CWR's vision is to enable people to experience personal transformation through applying God's Word to their lives and relationships.

Our Bible-based training and resources help people around the world to:
- Grow in their walk with God
- Understand and apply Scripture to their lives
- Resource themselves and their church
- Develop pastoral care and counselling skills
- Train for leadership
- Strengthen relationships, marriage and family life and much more.

Our insightful writers provide daily Bible reading notes and other resources for all ages, and our experienced course designers and presenters have gained an international reputation for excellence and effectiveness.

Our venue, Waverley Abbey House, provides excellent facilities in idyllic settings – ideal for both learning and spiritual refreshment.

CWR Applying God's Word
to everyday life and relationships

CWR, Waverley Abbey House,
Waverley Lane, Farnham,
Surrey GU9 8EP, UK

Telephone: **+44 (0)1252 784700**
Email: **info@cwr.org.uk**
Website: **www.cwr.org.uk**

Registered Charity No. 294387
Company Registration No. 1990308